Coming &
Going

Also by James J. McAuley

Coming & Going

New and Selected Poems

James J. McAuley

The University of Arkansas Press
Fayetteville   1989   London

DESIGNER: *Nancy Burris*
TYPEFACE: *Linotron 202 Sabon*
TYPESETTER: *G&S Typesetters, Inc.*
PRINTER: *Braun-Brumfield, Inc.*
BINDER: *Braun-Brumfield, Inc.*

The paper used in this publication meets the minimum
requirements of the American National Standard for
Permanence of Paper for Printed Library Materials
Z39.48-1984. ∞

Library of Congress Cataloging-in-Publication Data

McAuley, James J.
    Coming & going.
    I. Title. II. Title: Coming and going.
PR6025.A1612C6   1989   821'.914   88-29576
IBSN 1-55728-072-X (alk. paper)
ISBN 1-55728-073-8 (pbk. : alk. paper)

To the memory of Liam Miller, d. May, 1987, who revived, almost singlehandedly, the art of the finely-made book which had flourished in Dublin in previous ages; and who brought into print, and kept in print, the work of virtually a whole generation of Irish poets.

The friendship and generosity of spirit Liam offered me for over a quarter of a century I will never forget.

Beannacht Dé ar a anaim.

CONTENTS

ACKNOWLEDGMENTS

Dolmen Press and Colin Smythe for poems from *Draft Balance Sheet* and *Recital*.

University of Missouri Press for poems reprinted from *After the Blizzard* by James J. McAuley, by permission of the University of Missouri Press. Copyright 1975 by James J. McAuley.

Confluence Press for *The Exile's Book of Hours*.

To the editors of the following periodicals:
Poetry Ireland Review: "The Exile on His Failing Vision" and "A Gesture."
Studies: "In the Red Corner."
Willow Springs: "Coming & Going."
Poetry Northwest: "Ten-Mile Run."
Running Briefs: "Running in Snow."
Calapooya Collage: "Aor against the Termagant . . ."; "Aor against the Philistine . . ."; "Three Acts from a Play."

"The Exile's Fifth Symphony" is from the sequence comprising *Praise!*, a theatre piece for orchestra, chorus, and tenor solo, music composed by Wendal Jones, which was performed by the Spokane Symphony Society, Michael Hume, soloist, at the Spokane Opera House in February, 1981.

"Aor against the Termagant . . ." also appears in *Illuminations* (Oxford, U.K.).

FROM
Draft Balance Sheet
1968−70

LECTURE

This morning, friends, the blackboard will be black
Behind my skull; your eyelids will be slack,
And I could wearily cajole from you, or you,
Slow answers to dull questions, or grow annoyed
Earnestly deploying in the black void
Lyra's measured stars. But I must learn anew
To cope with darkness: these voids won't do
For slate on which to plot the dusty lore,
The diagrams, the arty emblems you ignore,
Your blood too thin to tick into the brain
The winged horse mustered from the sod
To be the Muses' pet, a demi-god
High in black heaven. I will not strain—
The chalk crumbling, your lids flickering—to explain
Why ignorant men pricked darkness full of scars
And gave them godly names, and called them stars.
You quench whole constellations on the black
Walls of your skulls; arts you dishonor die;
The sky will go black and Hippocrene run dry
Before I will fix one light in your blind skulls this black
Morning, friends. The blackboard will stay black.

MAKING REPAIRS

with James Whitehead,
University of Arkansas, 1966–68

Vulcan is up there, hammering
With chiselled fist on a manuscript
As if it would yet make a weapon
For a war of gods; but forgetting
The war is over, lost
To Mammon's unfeeling host.

Icarus is down here, trying
To fix his wings, sighing
As the wax melts in the heat
Of his own hand. He cannot repeat
That first ecstasy of flight,
Or his first failure's bleak delight.

MAP

I

In six-inch scale, the Mayo baronies
Cover half the wall above my couch.
Bog and mountain, tarn and cascade: I trace
These abrupt crazed contours where the gannet sweeps
Round rock and cliff, the bay below groaning, the wind
Cudgelling the coarse grass flat as it drives inland.

Here, on the narrow slope between crags and sea,
Clan fought clan, the misty cliffs over them,
Searock a false step below, and the Atlantic gale
Drumming their shields with shafts of rain. No peace
Ever visits that shore; no worth in that stony ground.

II

Papers everywhere—piled onto tables and shelves—
Accounts marked overdue, old magazines, failed poems.
A room occupied too long. Inertia. I should
Give up scanning the map, prone here on the couch,
And like my father take rootless flight.

He was an inconstant collector—Spode jugs,
The *Complete Works of George Moore*, trout flies—
Fads, pawned off in time, to pay for new caprices.
In his last place, the apartment in Beirut,
He spread a dozen Persian rugs, overlapping each other,

Auctioned off after his death. I held on to
His bronze gesturing Shiva, with his little smile.
Has ancestral greed driven us over the earth . . . ?

III

Was it greed for possession of these salty crags
That drove them at each other, wave after wave,
Yelling and stumbling through bulrushes and mire
Between Achill and the Bellacorick marsh?
No one records the outcome, no one knows the victor:
Place of Great Slaughter, the name in Irish on the map.

> When the blighted stalks
> Lay cracked and brown above
> The harrow-rows, the lean
> Poets stopped their singing
> By the blackened hearth and sought
> The exile ship in the cove,
> Or death released them from
> Mourning the pestilence
> That shadowed every face,
> And rage against the tyrant
> Whose greed fostered famine
> Rattled in their throats.

IV

Rage swept them across the Vistula, Danube, Elbe,
Before they had names for rivers. They hammered
Images into bronze and gold to shield them
For the crossing to the Isles of Bliss they dreamt
Beyond the storms. Now they have spanned oceans
And given their names to places they stayed in
Hardly long enough to light a fire or dig a grave.

6

My father learned to navigate the old way,
By the stars—could fly a course
From Ganges to Euphrates—knew half the globe
From the air. The Ides of March: taking off
From Tehran, his plane crashed at the edge
Of a place that is called in Persian *Desert of Salt.*

"Twenty thousand feet above the Aegean,
Setting course for Alexandria. . . .
If you can get to Basel I can meet you
And take you on to Beirut." His letter folded
Round the cash for the fare, but I bought instead
A box of secondhand books, and stayed home
In a littered room, to doze to Haydn; to put down
The pen, lost for words, considering the map,
The pibroch sounding, the warriors shouting.

> The gannet settles
> On a narrow ledge
> Between rowdy waves
> And rain-laden clouds.
> On the slope of great slaughter
> A mountain ash raises
> Its one stricken limb.

In memory of my father,
Capt. J. Noel McAuley,
1908–1963

SOLILOQUY

When my madness comes
As it will   it will
Unfastening the face
Hands dropping limp
When my madness comes
I will accept its curse
Keep a grip on failure
For man   house   machine
Must fail when controls
Unmesh and articulation
Grinds out its logic   I will know
When my madness comes
From their effects the words
Have lost connection

I stay   I stay   in my fear
When my madness comes
Rising through the heart's
Dark cells   and I feel it swell
Through veins   nerves   brain and sweep
All reason on its flood   and seethe
Against tooth and tongue when
My madness comes

DRAFT BALANCE SHEET

A shambling urban prospect
Spreads under gathering clouds.
Pale grass climbs through derelict beams,
Breaks from old basement flagstones,
Advances over scarred ground.

New movement of men and gear
Will throw up girder and glass.
In the hoarding's shadow, a slick wind
Plucks at discarded wrappings, crumpled foil,
Flicks over gleaming rubbish.

Clouds build like Atlantic rollers
Over the street's sad scape. I turn my back
On the view that hardly a month ago
Stretched a Palladian vista to the Dublin hills.
The heart won't ease: what use are these few lines?

Nothing I scribble down accounts for leaving:
The tickets are bought for the journey—but a month's rent paid—
Our lot improves if we emigrate—our wings to spread—
And yet the aching for home burns as if home
Had been across water these past twenty years.

The skyline climbs against the dropping sun.
Bridges arch dun water; the city's only
Skyscraper strikes up from the Liffey wall.
Old rooftops gather westward, black and sheer
Across the red-gold sky like sea-carved rocks.

Streetlights flare along the quays and tumble
Like yellow flags churning in murky water
Past barracks, breweries, brothels, old domes,
Past the Ballast Office, the Custom House, and out
Past Bailey's winking light to the dark sea.

The train grinds round the loopline over the bridge.
We rumble through drizzle: the cemetery wall,
The drenched bog. We pick up speed between stations
As misgivings mount in the heart. Then grey
Galway stone. Then the launch out to the liner.

A final panorama: village lights
Pinned on the low receding coast like moths;
Connemara frets the sky that glows
Faintly, even near midnight. Then all is sea.
Drunk exiles sing, and the great ship rises
Near Aranmore, lit up like a Disney palace.

The stewards are blond Norwegians; passengers
From Denmark, New York, Berlin. We're under way,
And the heave of ocean in a force-eight gale
Drives me sick to my cabin. These days, these years,
And the land exacts her tribute: this rage, this love.

FROM

After the Blizzard

1970—75

THE EXAMINATION

You make me dizzy with lust.
Watching as you write,
Ballpoint alive in your fist,
The line so delicate
From breast to palpable breast,
I'm making an estimate
Of how much you'd invest
(No time to meditate!)
Of thrust and counterthrust
If we should share a sheet.

Your fingers tire, resist
The throbbing pen. You're stiff.
You stretch. This easy test
On *Medea* brings you grief.
With all these treasures blessed,
You still will make an F.

THE ACTOR: DECLINE AND DEATH

We called him by his family name, one known
Throughout our tortuous history. He sat
His café chair like a throne or charger, speaking
Treason, biting a *croissant,* glancing quickly
From a round unwrinkled face at each of us,
His throaty laughter inviting us to join.

We applauded loudly from our balcony seats
The night he growled his notorious curtain speech
Mocking the senators. A blue vein quickened
At his temple later, as he joked with us
Hoarsely at supper. To our concern, his rejoinder:
Arrest me? I'm no danger. But with them, who knows?

At those *soirées,* while the witty speakers
Were taking his part, he downed his brandy too quickly,
And glowered round the table. When he had hushed our
Chatter, he quoted Cicero enjoining
Vigilance, and mimicked the leaders we knew
Wished his death. *Weak men! They'll be unseated.*

After his release, we found him once with the quick
Park pigeons bowing to his feet. When we
Approached his bench, he stood. His stiff joints
Made him groan; we thought he dissembled, knowing
How thoroughly every character entered and sat
Enthroned in his head, dictating what he spoke.

Bars of light sliced the long bare ward, where we
Were his only visitors. He had rejoined
The commonalty, his face a mask none would know
But the handful of schoolchildren who had been sitting
Close to the stage when he played Lear. He'd spoken
Faintly of filial treachery, then stepped back quickly,

Collapsing into the Fool's lap. . . . Hands joined
On the quiet breast; eyes not quite closed. Who could know
What vision kept him silent? Death sat
In the broken harp of his larynx, a dark unspoken
Syllable, one he would love to utter in his quick
Ironic growl, sharing the joke with us.

Now we're no longer so quick-witted, and seldom sit
In the cafés together, speaking of him. We know
We are soon to join him. Waiting subdues us.

THE EXILE'S RECURRING NIGHTMARE

I Prologue.

Not for me, the crusader cross:
I carry the common badge
Of exile, an uneven wedge
Of geese wild on a field of loss,
Legend: MEA CULPA on its edge.

> Desert, strewn with rock.
> In the tawny dust, my own track.
> The sun's unblinking eye.
> Then ahead, white wings sweep
> Up, lifting, lifted. *Go back,*
> *Go back,* I heard their wild cry,
> Nor woke from that troubled sleep.

II Memoirs of a Son of Erin.

THE ISLAND

My Lady of the Rocks,
The yachtsman's laughing daughter!

Behind the harbor, where sharp rocks
Gnashed their teeth at low cloud
Rushing to sea on a fair breeze,
She found the one smooth place
And sat enthroned. On the shore,
No more than a cast of the crab-line away,

I kept my place below her,
Spying, as she laughed,
Throwing her head back, laughing,
Her shadowy cleft. Cruel God!
Threaded by that thin green line
Angling down to the grey sea's floor,
I feared God would send a great Crab
To fasten on my baited hook
And drag me to damnation
For longing that my Lady
Of the Rocks would laugh, parting her thighs
Under her holiday skirt—
I would sail on her father's ketch
Past Rockabill and Lambay
To the ends of the earth, lusting
After my Lady of the Rocks!

THE NATION

Here stood Saint Anne's, seat of the Plunkets.
Sleek horses cantered in pasture, the sea-breeze;
A prospect of Howth through lilac and forsythia;
Set for an idyll by Watteau, the belvedere.

The old Count, a champion of cooperatives,
Sat in the first Dáil. The Free State
Commandeered the house, a Palladian gem
Which a drunken quartermaster burned down
To conceal his paltry embezzlements.

The hawser twangs taut: the tractor prowls
Backward over the broken terrace. The great
Gable wall groans, bricks spill. Fire-blackened,
A plaster cherub rides over rubble, plunges.

THE CHURCH

Bishop Patrick slew a goat in this holy village.
Born under that horned sign: shriven in that saint's church.

The sacristan swung us high on the knotted bell-rope
When he rang the angelus out over town and tide.

We brought the old cripple food vouchers, a blanket.
Her cabin stank of excrement, gangrene. She cursed us.

Our Holy Mother the Church is the haughty nun
Whose steel-rimmed spectacles flash, whose pearl
Rosary-beads clink in the black folds of her crotch.

III   Journey with a Conjuror.

That prodigal road! By rampant hawthorns you braked
The noisy pre-war Adler, and we walked
Out on the bridge below the salmon-weir.
Blue-black fish arched, their silver bellies flashed
And smacked into foamy brown water. The horned Norse
Tried the river this far: Leixlip, they named this glade.
As we left, two frowning swans took command.

In Kinnegad, a barmaid gone on magic.
You told this lass of a thousand calf-eyed smiles
A wedding-night joke; palmed a coin and plucked it
From behind her jewelled ear. She whimpered
With delight. For breakfast, she brought goatsmilk
And fat speckled eggs she stole herself from the nest.

Donegal roared: a great gale threw white spume
Against black cove-mouth rocks and low
Cottages hunched in the wind. For three full days
The Atlantic boomed round the empty hotel. We talked
Over stout and brandy about women, and Desire
Danced in our cigar-smoke round the varnished lounge.
The shy waitress, thin and plain, was transformed
To a priestess of venery.
                              The third day, we arose

To clearing weather, and Errigal's hoary cone
Stolid as lust ahead of us over the bog.

IV   The Whiskey Priest Recites His Holy Office.

MATINS

Beast-head in the mirror:
Goat without horns, Amen.
Thread of blood in my spittle.

Song of blame, song of loss
Hums like beating wings
In this skull, but won't pass these lips.

Hic est enim sherry for breakfast.
This shaking is my body.
They have stretched cords to snare my feet.

TENEBRAE

Darkness heaves and spins.
I am at some edge.
A wild wing sweeps up.

My own breath: *Ho!*
This dark is memory.
I stretch my arms full, so.

The void's at the tip of my fingers.
I will my flesh to remember.
Sweat crawls on my thigh.

What sound takes shape in the throat?
Oh, low the word I'd sing,
Were I to sing.

VESPERS

In that desert dream, I stared
A long time at the place
Burned black by those white wings.

Beside the bed, near enough,
The overturned glass, empty.
A stain like blood on the floor.

The same dream, the same dream.
That cluster of rocks, that cairn
Marked nothing, cast no shadow. I kept

Watch through the night without darkness.
There! in the yellow dust,
My track turned back from the edge.

And out of great fear I awoke.

PENANCE

for Owen

Tonight with the full green moon
Sliding down the pane
And you bawling a stubborn hour
From your cot till I put the fear
Of the devil in you with a roar—
This, that I might atone
For my sinful yell, or have power
To stay your cries
And close your eyes:

Pardon, child, your father, who made
A demon in his own likeness, a toad
Bellowing like a bison, to frighten
You down to nightmare. How can I brighten
The dark that makes you sob? Listen:
Here, where the moon looks in through
Your Punch-and-Judy window,
I'm knocked flat by a cackling elf—
See how his big eyes glisten?
He whistles through his nose like this, and
His long white whiskers bristle—
When he kisses you they tickle—
Well? Have I redeemed myself?

SUNFLOWERS: AN ODE

I

Beyond the crowding spires of pine, the hill
Curves down to Meadow Lake. The village street
Drags its houses one by one into stubble fields.
Finch cries to finch on boughs
That dip their leaves to the roof.
The sky is a blue eyelid; odor of bones in the loam
I turn into the sun with my spade.

Clay yields to root, a branch cracks in a storm,
And what is it to me? I can bend low
Over the ready ground and push seed down
With my thumb; or sit idle
On the doorstep watching sparrows
Build a nest in the birdhouse on the half-dead cottonwood.
Here, earth and air are full of promises.

II

I planned a little fountain
Dropping over pebbles,
Warbling a simple *allegro*.
But the mortar cracked, the water seeped away.
Here is its stony promise.

I planted lavender, white heather,
Memories of an Irish garden.
But this soil is too bitter.

Not one frond grew to scent the dusk.
Here are their names, their images.

Mowing the lawn, the machine
Growling, shuddering, reducing all
To a flat green, I found
The sparrow's egg under the cottonwood.
Here is its perfect speckled oval.

III

I lounge on the warm step, watching the child
Asleep in his cradle. A spotted butterfly
Crosses the lawn like an affectionate memory.

Above the fence they rise in strict green rows,
Leaves broadening on their muscular stems,
Bees making their summer pilgrimages.

Soon their aureoles will ride
High above the weeds where the lavender failed,
A yellow galaxy beyond the crumbling fountain,

Soon to stand trembling in the August heat,
Then bend in the Fall winds, bend to spill their seed.
And when the first frost blackens their stiff heads,
I will go among them and flatten them back to the ground.

MNEMOSYNE: THE EMPTY ROOM

for Dick Case

A woman rises naked from the bed,
Drags off the filthy coverlet.
A woman's heavy torso rising, bending.
She holds her fleshy stomach, looking down
At her bony hands, her flaccid thighs, her mound.
A woman, naked, unable to weep or reproach you.
You watched her awake and rise. Why will she not weep?

The stench of liquor. You reach down
Under the bed, the side
Away from the woman. Your thin
Left arm is all that moves now.
The stench is brimstone. The glass is cold, cold.
Your hand bends round it. Wormwood. The woman goes.
You lean forward, and carry it to your lips,
Slow, careful. You drink.

Cough. Shudder. Choke on the foul wine.
Try again to drink. Again. Weep for her.
Cry out to the yellow sunlight in the window,
Cry to the crumpled ghost in your clothes
Crawling vomit-stained across the bare floor.
Cry to your comrades, astir in the other rooms,
Beginning the same ritual, shivering, teeth grinding.
Cry till you are breathless. Empty the glass.

The woman will return, stand over you,
Her molten flesh alight in the yellow beam.
She'll finger your limp parts, press herself
Down on your loins. It will take long
For you to be consumed by her caress.

VIVALDI IN VENICE

(La Cetra, op. 9)

I

Arched corridors. Bare white walls.
Sunlight slants off water, dapples
The Pietà by the chapel door.
The dead Redeemer's hand
Is glossy from pious stroking.

The girls in grey uniforms, bows
Poised over their polished viols,
Whisper in the great vaulted room
Where waterlight dapples the ceiling.
Under their lowered eyelids, sins
Unnumbered. The redhaired *maestro,*
Hand raised as for a blessing,
Smiles, "Begin."

II

Violas are moaning, a harpsichord chiming
Chords he made simply to please.
The Emperor nods like Apollo,
Lulled by the resonant cellos.
Divine violin,
Sing low, sing in;
To orphan, to emperor, bring heartsease,
In court and convent redeeming,
Redeeming sin.

III

Under the humming *continuo,*
The needle sits on the whispering disc.
The globe keeps its face to the sun,
The sun-god's golden lyre
Leads orphan Ophelia singing.
Nodding, humming, the last
Hapsburg surveys the salon,
The rustling, charmed ambassadors.

The needle sticks on a high note,
A strange bleating repeated.
The smiling, clouded, stops.
Sin, Madness, Grief
Enter, screeching and screeching.

BALDUNGAN CASTLE

for Michael

A hard climb. Worn flag steps,
Steep, slippery. Thick walls sweated
In the spiralling dark. Then bright
Sun on the narrow parapet.

What passed between us there,
On Baldungan's height?
Sun on ripe wheat in the fields,
On the sea we could scarcely hear,

On the familiar ground
That in our blood we could feel
Close by: inlets, islands, rocks,
The harbors of two grey towns.

From their nests in the embrasures,
Round us the bickering rooks,
Abusing us, circling the keep
Encircled by our places:

Rush, Skerries, Santry, Naas.
Naas. Rush. Graves there keep
Mother and father, for good
Or ill, separate.

You vaulted the five-bar gate
To the field below the keep;
Broke off wheat-ears; rubbed
Them in your hands, shared the grain.

Touring the grey towns, we stood
Each other many drinks. They keep
Fine whiskey in those places. Late
That night, we quarrelled again.

AFTER THE BLIZZARD

I

The air of an old song's in my head.
Wind puffs at the snow, sifting it
Into fences, tree trunks, walls.
Straight above, a pale star winks out
In a clear streak of brightening sky.

Clouds pace over the house,
Making east with their burden.
Far down the hemisphere, light
Spreads between the clouds
As a door would open slowly
On a room left long disused.

What brought me here through the house?
You and the children sleep
Where still the dark is right.
Old tune, words faded, keeps
Pushing breath to my lips.

II

Behind a brightening cloud
The sun begins to climb
The low winter path
That will take it scarcely above
That crowd of swaying pines.

I cannot remember the name
Of the star above my house.
You and our sleeping sons
Are for a moment nameless, gone.
My song dies, the notes melting.
Breath is mist in cold air.

The garden lies deep under snow.
Shadows return from the dead
As the light grows. A dead bough
Angles up, a black arm
Out of snow, parting the gold cloud.

III

Not a sound. The house could be
A dark ship locked in snow
And I her captain, my breath
Spangled in strange light.

Where is the hawk and his victim?
Where is the mole and the cat
That will devour him? The snow
Swept down through the dark

With the same power that made
The star grow pale and leave
The sky; quiet as the breath
Of my nameless song on the glass.

A bird off in the pine-wood
Pipes one high note.
The house is dark and quiet.
I remember a line from the song:

Where'er you tread,
The blushing flow'rs shall rise.

A song for summer. Time
To turn back through the house,

Ease open the door
Where the children sleep, their breath
Like wind in snow. The light
Grows pale gold at their window.

SIGNS

Cowboy gear hangs from smoky beams: the Colt
In its holster, bright metal and glossy leather;
The long rifle with the shiny trigger; shiny spurs.
A crimson garter. A bronze pool trophy. And signs:
CREDIT TO EIGHTY-YEAR-OLDS WITH THEIR PARENTS CONSENT.
THE SADDLE INN branded on a polished board.
The owner wears a buckskin jacket; a new joke
With a bawdy punchline, every time I'm here.
Blacks, Jews, Poles, Irish are all fair game.

Grace, his wife, is soft-spoken, smiles mostly,
Knitting for a grandchild or drawing beer
From the gleaming taps under the owner's photo
In its toilet-seat frame. Behind her on a shelf
THE PERFECT BIRTH-CONTROL PILL is a big white disk.
HOLD FIRMLY BETWEEN THE KNEES, the directions say.

The sergeant from the airbase and his wife
Breeze through the door where the silver horseshoe glitters.
He is fat and hearty. His wife's a doll.
Over the narrow door marked GENTS, a pair
Of mannequin legs thrust out from the wall like antlers.

The sergeant's wife plays pool, tapping the cue-tip
On her gleaming teeth as she figures her shot. There's a mock-
Official sign nailed to the lavatory door:
IN CASE OF NUCLEAR ATTACK, 1. REMOVE
ALL SHARP OBJECTS. 2. PLACE HEAD
BETWEEN THE KNEES. and 3. KISS ASS GOODBYE.

CARUSO

From the scratchy past his voice
Spirals up to a high note;
The aria rises, swells;
The orchestra storms like the last
Judgment, and song throbs
In my own throat, a great breath
Held in the lungs, ready
To ease out that long high note.

I will stride out, Pagliacci,
Plant my feet on the pavement—
Dead lawns, powerlines, clamped
Boulevards—throw my arms wide—
And their houses will break open like chrysalids,
Gaspumps will blossom like orchids—
I will lift my face to the ashen sky
And give my whole body to song—

Housewives will rub their hands on their aprons,
Tenors with samplecases, wrenches, trays of drinks,
Portly *bassos* from insurance agencies,
Sopranos from beauty-salons, ruddy boys
In grubby denim from weedy playgrounds—
They too will take stance in the street,
Ready for *Va Pensiero,* or Mahler's
Veni Creator Spiritus—their world
Carried away to the blue eternal hum
With Caruso's last long note.

DUST-DEVILS

Drought. Grey spirals into hard blue
Seventy feet or more from over Harding's field,
The dust he plowed last week, sticking to schedule
Even when the seasons don't. Come Sunday, it'll be
Ninety days and nights and hardly a cloud,
Never mind rain. In June a front went over,
Not a drop, but lightning fired the forest
West of town, pillars of flame in tall rows,
Rocks cracking wide in the heat, and the smoke
Thick as wool for three full days. Preacher said
The sweet dry stench of burn that kept the town
Making sour faces and coughing was surely of hell.

Yesterday, on the old country road, no more than ten
Feet ahead of the pickup, we watched one start
From nothing, rattling old cans in the ditch.
It swept across the old Metlock place, spun out
In the black-locust grove round the ruined house.
Harmless. You could stand in one, it would tease your hair.
Bad sign, though, dry earth, dry air, dancing together.
On the reservation over the river, they're counted
The spirits of dead braves, still seeking peace.

Nothing to be done with our scrub land
But ride fence in the pickup, bouncing hard ground,
Trailing our plume of dust. In dry waterholes,
Our steps make small puffs, though we move slow.
Found a dead calf in the creek bed: brown hide,
Pale bones showing through, flesh and insides gone.

Dust powdered over the carcass by struggling coyotes.
Every night, they howl closer to the house.
Old Stan, our wino hand, shivers at their sound.

I dream nights of those burning trees, the shouts
Of the firefighters; wake with a dry throat. Metlock
Quit his farm, they say, because he dreamt the house
He built of pine logs he cut himself was crushed
Under black boulders that grew from the seed he spread.
He dreamt of this, night after night; then drove off
From that solid house. It took ten years for the roof
To collapse in the snows of 'sixty-seven.
They say Harding will be the next to fail, the stubborn
Fool, scattering seed and fertilizer on dust.
I'll stay, though the preacher scolds every Sunday of hell,
Of our sins turning the fields into the devil's playground.

GREEN BEER

I

On Saint Paddy's Day, the jukebox plays
Bing Crosby singing "Galway Bay,"
And the color TV in this friendly dive
Is freckled with kilted dancers, live
Little dolls with their jigs and reels
Between the commercials for stomach pills.

The barman slides me another beer.
"On the house, Irish." "Good to be here."
He asks me—they all ask—what I think.
I assure him the situation stinks.
"The murther and mayhem over there
Is somethin' a body can hardly bear,"
My brogue as phony as the beer is green.
The barman tops her up again.
The Gaelic lassies from the Bronx
Blur and fade as they end their dance.

II

I dream a flag snaps in a cold wind:
The Plough-stars in gold on a blue ground,
Blurred by smoke. Kneeling beneath,
A shadow, on watch: an armed youth,
Fist clenched over the burning town.
Into the red sky creeps a false dawn.
Then dead Cuchulain bound to the tree,
And the raven stabbing his eye.

THE PATH

". . . and when I speak, the images of all I speak of
are present, out of the same treasury of memory;
nor would I speak of any thereof, were the images
wanting."

—St. Augustine.

So began our one flirtation with winter:
Fiery eyes in a bush
Fleshed by our lights.
The dark way home brought us to that white edge.

The beast that watches lovers and curses them:
An old rage, a blunt pulse
In the brain, drove us
To rage at dark and cold. Its track roved free everywhere.

A black form on the long ridge of Wright's Hill,
Haunched like an idol
Against the low clouds,
Stayed still as hunter or hunted when we passed,
Steering between high banks
Of drifted snow. One night
It attacked, leaping at our lights, eyes
Burning as it fell away
Rolling, scrabbling on ice.
Then the limitless white silence returned to path and hill.

The old ones told
Us what to do.
"Kill it, track it down to its lair, its young
Too, kill them, kill."
We remembered its eyes.
One, very old, blind, neither woman nor man,
Said nothing, hands

Stretched to the flames.
A widow fed small twigs, one by one, to the fire.
Heavy snow that night.
Going home, we saw
Its fresh trail beside the treacherous road.

The long line of men and youths abreast,
Black ciphers in the snow,
Hallooed, whistled, yapped
Like pups. None would give it an assured name,
Nor believe in more than one.
Our voices rang in cold air.
The spoor gave out in the windblown ice of the lake.

The women began to feel,
In the blood of lovers and sons,
The beast of the blazing eyes, hunter and hunted.
Old paths from house to house
Grew faint beneath new snow.
No one claimed to have seen it; only its tracks.
At last the blind one
Growled from the hearth:
"It will be there forever. You cannot live without it."

That was our one flirtation with the winter.
After the thaw, our cars,
Lights chewing tracks
Through the dark, sped the highways between our cities.
We named the animals,
Set names for everything,
Even for what made our hearts race as we passed
Through the dark
Beyond our lights.

FOR THE HUMANISM CLASS AT FAIRCHILD AIRFORCE BASE, IN PLACE OF A SESSION ON THE BOOK OF JOB

"O remember that my life is wind: mine eyes shall no more see good."

—Job 7:7

Sunset. Look away to the airbase, far
At the western edge of the parched plain.
Stolid Stonehenge could tell time no better:
Sheer black slabs stand up to the red
Wall of the sky. Close in. Speed up.

From Rambo Road they grow to great
Black bomber fins, alert on the ramp,
Alert in their circle, awaiting the last
Word. Slow down. Look away: look east
To the fallow field, to the moorhen squatting
On her nest in the reeds by the pond's edge.

Pick up speed. Look ahead. Switch on
Lights. Check the controls, the green
Dials glowing, my hand easy
On the wheel. Easy, easy to rise
High into whistling ether, to bank and roll
Over the darkening globe, to leave below
The black bird on her nest, the black
Circle of fins; to set course
Straight for the sun's red diameter.

Down in the headlights
A grey blur, a slight
Creature. A squirrel. Brake.
Too late, Stop. Look back.

All gravity brings me too late
To the body flattened, the head
Moving, alive. It looks straight
At me in the tail-light's red
Glow. Take a stick
From the ditch and strike
Till the small black eyes glaze dead.

Look away, look away. All quiet
On the ramp where the bombers squat.
The motor hums under the hood.
In gear. Pick up speed. Look ahead.

WITNESS

"Sometimes the witness is more strangely involved than the actor."
—George Garrett, *King Of The Mountain*

I

What did she see on the train?
Two figures, blurred by speed.
Light from a flashing sign,
Or the flash of a driven blade?
Was there a victim mouth
Hollowed out by pain,
The other figure crouched,
Ready to strike again?

II

She felt, as she left the station,
Those shadows move in her head
From confusion to conviction:
The victim pale, half-dead,
As the flushed assailant hurried
Through the platform crowd. . . .
She'd often seen these lurid
Murder scenes: The screen showed
The shadowy act carried out
In ways that left no doubt. . . .

So when two men, laughing, squabbling,
Shouldered through the rumbling
Station behind her, she knew
Them as killer and victim, and grew

42

Wild-eyed, a Cassandra, babbling
Over and over, "I saw! I saw!"

III

Had I been at that scene,
Watching the weak in their vain
Struggle with the strong,
I wouldn't have been long
Staring at the whole
Masquerade before pale
Complexions of the damned,
Murderous gestures, framed
In fiercest colors, would reel
Through the brain a tale
So ancient and cruel—such a lie
As to transfigure all who passed by.

QUESTIONS FOR MY GRANDFATHER

First, apologies, as usual,
For not writing this long while.
Our family's not too close;
Why's that, do you suppose?
Well, now. Do you still live
In that snug house, like a cave
Hidden behind its big sycamore?
(Or is that an oak by the door?)

Is the old humpback Ford
Still in the garage? What bush
Hides this year's nesting thrush?
In September, will you hoard
Apples and pears again
In wardrobe drawers, to send
At Hallowe'en as rewards
For good great-grandchildren?
How often do they drop in
To see you? Or do they forget, bored
By that sunny oldfashioned room?
Is it still in its frame,

That photo of you and my father,
On the mantel? (Or the piano?)
He begs a loan: you pretend *No*.
I swear, you were the image of each other!

At family cards—all those
Games!—the lamp behind you,

Your pokerface in shadow,
Why did you let yourself lose?

Do you still walk the park
With Mack, your Kerry-Blue,
Stiffly at heel beside you?
When the gatelatch clicks,
Will he, as usual, bark,
If I come to pay my respects?

FROM
Recital
1975−82

RITUAL

Before I offer the wood,
I whet the knife on a stone
With simple strokes, back and forth,
So. I disown these hands,
Empowered by laws that hold
Moon and tide to their pledge.
Steel and stone, flesh and bone,
The blade's light song repeats.
I test its edge on the stony
Heel of my hand before
I offer the wood to the knife.

I learn again to take pains
With simple things: to take
The knife in my better hand, so;
And the driftwood, already worn
By the steely waves to a shape
I recognize as if dreamt
While I rocked in those waves myself—
The wood in this hand, so.

The mask of one I recognize
Stares up from the wood. I begin.

THE CONFESSION

To the grey rock below the silent park, in grey light,
The tide in its patient blind labor has yielded up
The girl's body, so waxen-white and rigid now

She could no longer drive her lover to this murder,
Nor excite the youth who found her stretched there and is held
Fast by unearthly fear, having once and for all

Discovered the mystery of the flesh. With his coat
He has covered her, so she seems a Shrovetide effigy
Cast into the sea at midnight when revellers turn

Penitent. In the Bayview Condominium,
Shadows waver behind the venetian blinds;
Roused early from their beds by the siren, a few

Emerge on their verandahs, in bathrobes, hugging themselves,
Watching through opera-glasses while a doctor kneels
To hold her wrist, shaking his head, and the sky

Stealthily brightens. The detective stares at the sea,
Having pulled the boy's coat away. The coroner stands aside, and she
Is suddenly in focus. They lower the glasses and vanish inside,

Shivering. Her lover regards his hands as if another's
Clenched and unclenched before him, remembering
The low sound in her throat when her body opened

For love. He will never make the detective understand
How, cherishing her every breath, he surrendered
All that torment and desire to the quiet waves.

STUDIES FOR A SELF-PORTRAIT AT FORTY

I

You'd hardly notice at first how everything
Has been arranged in fours—geraniums
In red clusters—and how dark surfaces gleam:
Onyx ashtrays, brass candelabra, the table
Where white envelopes lie. Tempting, to chop
The thumbs from the hands that shuffle the letters,
And bury them under the cherry-tree outside,
All brightness round, their coffin a cedar
Cigarette-box from the Levant, inlaid
With the ivory figure of a woman—my mother, say,
Soon after my conception; or the nurse
Who sang while she washed my genitals
When I had scarlet fever. The envelopes
Murmur politely, saying my name four times.

II

Cock the right eyebrow: Heredity.
The self-mocker I try to surprise
In the mirror gets a laugh
Out of this repeated peering.

Tempting, to wear the black
Hat with the wide brim, clipped
Moustache, eyes narrowed in cunning.
One self is all art.

III Episodes for a Panel

A whiteskinned boy, halfdrowned,
On a gravel beach, his open
Mouth a black rictus. Later,
He could recall filtered grey
Light rising over him the third
Time he sank. Since then,

Nothing has begun or ended: he
Pushed through a dappled
Watery continuum as his feet
Lifted him along the seabed
The few yards to dry sand.

❖

Skinny youth in a garden perspective:
Yews form a nave for statues
Of skinny militant saints.
Loyola and Gonzaga guard
The shrine to the Virgin; he kneels
At the hem of the marble robe.
Her marble bosom swells; he prays
From his mouth, his thoughts all lust.

❖

Plump, shaved, hair cropped, he sits
On the edge of his hospital bed.
A plump, rosy nurse has suffered
His fingers to open her stiff
Uniform, to kiss the perfumed breast
She consecrates to Jesus
Every morning. Even her smile
Has been trained. He is wide-eyed,
Frowning. This tableau is joyless.

❖

Leathery, hirsute, he's the critic
Who stands with his didactic tweed
Sleeve raised in a gallery

Of *fin-de-siècle* portraits
By John Yeats, Lavery, Osborne.

The thoughtful figures converse
With each other over his head.
In this place too, he is frowning:
Mouth a black ridge, one hand pocketed.

IV

Better the big NOW, singular,
No symbolic trappings,
No sad accomplices.
Dante's dark wood hinted
Behind the left shoulder? Or,
From his next simile, grey
Seas, a thin wash to signal
Escape from drowning? Hello, Lazarus.

In this I have my father's features,
Though with a rime of beard on the cleft chin,
And my mother's eyes. I look my age.
Behind me on every side, grey seas
Wash against a northfacing shore,
All swept up in flat grey to the sky
It meets with a darker grey, and mottled
As lichen on stone. Leave it that way.

V

Leave the hair white, uncombed.
Change the eyes to suspicious,
Clamp the mouth thin as the line
Marking the horizon—leave that
To suggest escape from madness.

Open the thin mouth a little,
As if speech could not be stopped
While the pose held long enough
For the head to imply the skull's threat.

Hang this, even unfinished,
On a bare wall, and ask
What its subject was asking
While he waited for the shapes
Beyond him to be revealed.

Wait: change the mouth. And the forehead.
Make him pale, to hint at fear
And regret. Change the eyes: they
Look out at nothing. Now,
It will do. It will have to do.

LETTER TO RICHARD HUGO
FROM DRUMCLIFF

Dear Dick, This kind of travel is cheap enough:
Hard a'starboard after a vexing nightmare,
And there I leave you—Mister Yeats at Coole,
Being severe with young poets on Lady Gregory's lawn,
Looking over his shoulder at a few bedraggled sheep,
On the shore of the murky lake . . . and he counting them *swans!*

It's just a Byzantine canter through Roscommon,
By entailed estates and tinker camps, to Drumcliff.
A Philip Larkin chapel, half-buried in half-dead elms;
Bland Gothic of the Established Faith
That none of the neighbors gave a damn about,
Keeping to their long-lipped superstitions,
Their gutteral gossip making a natural prey
Of the poet's ancestral rector: ". . . a nice man, *but* . . ."
Half-starved mongrels worrying a lame sheep.

The embattled cleric: he patrols his neat grounds,
Pondering his fingernails, the only clean
Set in the parish; he's prepared to preach
On "Prudence" again to his congregation of five—
Six, if you count the deaf-mute poorhouse orphan,
His only convert, who rings the communion bell
And keeps the gentry's graves clear of weeds.

The peasantry: the poems depicted them vain
And cruel, dour and quaint; the poet went sour
On them, invented a freckled ghost in tweed
With a fly-rod and an ear cold enough

To hear him out. He caught neither salmon nor trout
Himself; hated low bars; all the women he loved
Had double-barrelled names—how could we common folk
Move in his goddam gyres, except *away?*

Randy laughter, hell! His lightest rhyme
Was strictly Big House—a bronze gong embossed
With moon, rose, rood, tower, and winding stair;
He struck well, and that great gong called
The lords and ladies to their place: stage *right.*
He warped the local colors of many a *rann*
To his own passionate, visionary weft,
As Vergil had for Rome in *her* decline.
Here, beneath white gravel, his bone-white grin.

At the top of the graveyard lane, on an old cross,
The disproportionate head of a crucified figure
Wears the same dissembling agony-smile.
Some nameless monk, ten centuries ago,
Chipped the lichen off a great rock and cut
Him down to size.
So, the gorgeous gong resounds through Idaho:
Here, the visitor looks up from where he lies,
His arrogant plain stone, to a croaking rook
Flapping out of a galebent hazel. It's like
Getting pissed off at Xerxes, as you say. Best, Jim.

TO HIS HOST,
WHO HAS ASKED HIM TO STAY LONGER

We've learned in hard ways when we have to go.
There's nothing to explain, no one to blame,
And so much still to learn, we joke in sorrow.
Our children leave the house before their time,
Without a quarrel, casual, taking with them
Nothing to prize, and we may never know
What names they'll give their children. Nothing to do
But keep the house as neat as a chapel nave,
Fondle our friends' wives, let the wine flow,
Dance to old records, crooning of life and love.

We're sprightly enough, God knows, till the first ones leave.
It's a new kind of politeness we've let grow,
Going home while the party's in full swing to save
Our oldest friends the shame of letting it show,
This waking weariness that lays us all so low.
Tortured in our own beds by a hopeless fury,
We harp on how in youth we were always merry,
But can't remember now what made us so.

CHEIRON

I

When I was a Curragh stableboy,
The filly Amaryllis sank
Her teeth in my shoulder as I bent
To ease her saddlegirth. This killed
In me the romance of these animals.

None of us without our mark from falls
Or rival whips—all of us deathsheads,
Lean as Hindu priests, awkward
As puppets when we walked the ground;
Many who learned nothing from their scars.

No horse I rode could fall. We took
Each fence for a prophecy to be
Fulfilled, into whose heart we galloped
Through the hallooing and cursing,
The boom of hooves, the inferno
Of gasp and snort, the bright flash of silk.

Then the breathless rocking
Over the cruel ditch, my fists
On the curving neck; then the tremor
Of landing, its head flung back
On the massive shoulder; and my head
There, steadying. Then the surge
Under my knees for the next impossible hurdle.

II

The young broke ribs and thighs, holding
To the old romance: great horse and gallant rider.
I offered what I knew, but they would not accept.
Older, the intense tragedians of too many seasons,
They turned an unquenchable rage on their mounts,
And drove them frothing at the fences until beast and man
Lay coupled in agony, thrashing the turf.

Once, launching over a laurel hedge at Phoenix Park,
I heard unearthly sobbing, then the scream
Of the broken-back horse
Before the steward's shot.

With all affection dead, I learned their powers.
I raced with the hope of winning, not to win.

III

To learn those powers, I surrendered
My claim to manhood. At the starting-gate,
I bent my head to that place
Behind the ear, where the snout
Of the merciful gun would press.

Listening for the starter's call, eyes closed,
Murmuring to calm my horse, I saw, clear
And familiar as dream, the course,
And, winning or losing, the way we would cover it.

And at the edge of that vision,
The others, their fearful chatter,
And their blurred colors: crimson,
Vermilion, cobalt, gold.

IV

I became a single sinew
Cleft to the galloping animal.
Once, three fences from home,
I pulled up just in time
On a gelding of Amaryllis'
Bloodline. But, winning or losing,
No horse I rode could fall.

AN IRISH BULL

*(An incongruous mixture of metaphors, often
unintentionally humorous, sometimes elusive or surreal,
originally rendered in a political context; a low
species of oratory, developed during the notorious
filibusters of Parnell's Irish Nationalist Party at
Westminster in the 1880's.)*

for James Whitehead, Aet. XL

Political passion is the poorest coin
We trade with. Slumped at the screen like resigned
Brokers or navigators, we're the last
To find direction out this way, or lend value to words
So debased in the common coinage, we feel them break
From their moorings in meaning when we bring them to meet

In metaphor—as if we could still make ends meet
Or tame any beast by such means. Words are coins
Thrown on a table to settle a debt, a sign
That nothing's settled.
                              In the news at last,
Franco is dead. The smart men give us the word:
"He was good for Spain." Then a commercial break.

Old Farrell, my countryman, twenty at the outbreak
Of that war when we both were born, went south to meet
A fascist slug that sent him home lame. No coin,
Spanish or Irish, could straighten his step, resigned
As he was in his hatred, his only desire to outlast
Those fanatical, bickering, stomachy men, whose word

Is good for Business, always a good word
With upstarts and fascists.
                              We've worked hard to break
Their code, to invest in a language that's meet;
But meanwhile the enemy we know has coined
A new name for himself, and left no sign
That's the least inimical, no word that lasts.

Rage in Belfast, Beirut, L.A. The last
News item, Dow Jones bullish; then a word
From our sponsor. The doldrums, without a break
In sight. In the boredom of bad news we meet
Our vilest enemy.
                            Better to toss a coin,
Tails for the fascists, sure to turn up, and resign

Ourselves like old Farrell to a cynicism designed
For our own good to bankrupt the spirit.
                                               The last
Word for them from the newsman leaves no word
Unturned: *Conservative!* Waves of falsehood break
Into froth to show us where these waters meet
The rocks we've sailed too close to.
                                          But if the coin

Flips up the imperious head of coins, could we assign
Politics a lasting language, find the exact words?
Or when the beast breaks loose, turn back to meet it?

THE EXILE TAKES STOCK
OF HIS SURROUNDINGS

How would we know who we are
If our names weren't engraved
On the mail-order napkin-rings?
We'd be extinct for generations
If it weren't that our souls
Live on in the bargains we hauled
Home from the discount stores:
The old slope-shouldered fridge,
The motor clucking like barnfowl,
A steal at forty bucks and a beer
Apiece for the husky sophomores
Who delivered it to our kitchen.
(One lemon has to go back:
The stereo—a pretty white cube
From Woolworth—makes Dvorak's
New World Symphony sound
Like soup spilled on a hotplate.)

Who will deliver us
From the food the kids won't eat,
The hotdogs bloody with ketchup,
Frenchfries like huge nailparings—
We should deliver the rest
Of the Minute Rice to Dacca—
Who will deliver us
From the empties stacked in the carport,
From the lamp that shorted and burned
When we plugged it in (*antique*,
The woman meant: *extinct*,

I heard her say, *Five*
Seventy-five as is but took
Two bits off for good will)—

Who will deliver us
From the blotched leaves on the plant
Dying in the window
Of the living-room behind
The yard-sale recliner
Still exuding disinfectant
And dead bugs on the rug
We bought from the Salvation Army—
Oh Lord, when they delivered
The diningroom suite, nothing down
And easy monthly payments—
Deliver us, deliver us
From the junkmail trumpetings
Of white sales, bargains, giveaways!

Our neighbor delivers the children
Home from the nursery school.
They fall asleep over dinner.
The pork'n'beans grow cold.
The TV glows blue-green
On their faces. (A good buy
At twenty-five bucks from Abilities
Unlimited. Works fine.)

REQUIEM

In memory of my mother, Maureen McAuley,
d. July, 1969.

In the memory of the dead
Is the consolation of the living

I   Mourners

The widow returns to the house
And accepts the quiet room,
The polished furniture.
Her hands rest in her lap.
She will soon find something to do
With her hands again. She says
His name aloud in the room.
❖
The one whose shoulder aches
From the weight of his sister's coffin
Has turned his back to the wind
To light a cigarette.
Flame hollows his skull;
Wind rips the smoke from his hands.
❖
The man whose wife is lying
Between the four tall candles
Waits for the women to leave,
Then climbs the stairs again
To quench the candles, one
By one. Then he sits all night
In the dark room beside her bed.

For the grieving are as numerous as the blades
Of the long reeds that bend in every wind,
Surviving, though their hollow roots hold sand.
As sorrow leaves us, so wind dies in the reeds.

II   "Alle Herrlichkeit des Menschen"

God of my childhood
Set free these dead
From the chains of my prayers

God of the light
That fixes this dead
Shadow to my heel

Make me in wisdom
Set free these dead
At last from my grief

III   Vigil

In my town the old sea-captain
Whose skin was sailcloth, whose speech
Was a gusty spittle, whose lies
Were crimson anemones that swayed
In the blue rockpools around
The green edge of my town—

In my town the captain was last
From his wrecked ship in a roaring
November storm—the breeches-buoy
Lifting him like a saint
Assumed into heaven over
The rocks and breakers, up the cliff
To the room with dim prints of ships

In full sail, where his pipe
Wheezed while he told me great lies.

In my town, at the rosary
The night they coffined him,
He was only another
Wheyfaced pensioner
Already gone straight to heaven
With the reek of Murray's Plug
Tobacco for a halo.
This was the first I'd seen
Of him with his weather eye closed.

IV   Glory

I sifted the coarse yellow sand
Through the hollow of my fist.
My heels dug inches in sand.
I bit on a reed from the dune
Where our loving had left its mark.
I tasted its salt. I made
Coarse music with it, a rasp—
The corncrake's misleading call.

The girl with me held wide
Her towel to show me her dark
Nipples, her silky dark pubes,
And covered herself again quickly.
Her laughter and my cry
Of shame and delight were flung
On the light wind over the bay.

Oh, survivors, who among you
Will grieve with me for those voices
Which die away in the whisper
Of small waves and the birds' piping?

V   Survivors

CHAPLAIN

Four shells on four yards
Of trench in the stripped wood
The Somme   July 1916
O *horrible   most horrible*
Trapped him in a dugout
With three fusiliers who cursed
Their bad luck first, but prayed
With him later, panting,
Words a flat hiss
On poison air.

The next barrage tore bright strips
From their eyes: the sky opened
Over the foul death-trench.
In gaseous day, in the childish
Whine of the unseen wounded, they joked
About the priest's hair, turned white
By that four hours' burial.

After the hospital morphine
They sent him to teach boys
Mathematics and History
Far behind the lines.
They let him grow dahlias and banks
Of rhododendron in the rich loam
Of the school's Pleasure Grounds.
The boys called him Thatch or Shakes
Behind his back; but they liked it
When he took them to help with his flowers.

BOMBARDIER

The youth who took
An ack-ack shard
Below the ribs
Was so fixed on
His bombsight that
He felt only a slight
Loosening

The plane kicked up
And banked for home
And he leaned away
From the silver threads
Of the railyard in
The crosshairs

BOMBS AWAY he
Yelled and reached
For a cigarette
Into the bowels
That filled his flight
Jacket he
Laughed and called
To the navigator
LOOK but the other
Was faceless dead

They sewed him back
Together but he kept
Asking for his old
Buddy   his navigator

SKIPPER

A cable winching boxes
Of mackerel out of the hold
Snapped and tore both thighs.
In the Harbor Bar he drank

From their bottle of pre-war cognac
While he waited for the doctor.

Castrate, and both legs lost,
He sold his brother the trawler
For half its worth. He wrote
On the back of a factor's docket:
God has laid his curse
Now I am half a man.

In a black storm, his brother
Ran the trawler on Shenick rocks.
The hull tore open like new bread.
His brother drowned; the crew
Brought off safe by the lifeboat.
For hours he shouted his brother's name
Into the flying spume, the luminous waves.
❖

For everywhere with their comrades are heroes who dare
To carry their grief as Achilles bore his shield,
With Patrocles lost, into the maddening war.
Sorrow is with them everywhere, the shadow at the heel.

VI   Creed

The rocks here, if they sang,
Would chant *Affirm! Affirm!*
They pile down from the cliff,
A great choir petrified
In the act of singing the canticle's
Sublime chord: *Amen!*

From the clifftop a summer forest
Spreads a green infinity
To meet the infinite blue
Of the sky that commands: *Affirm!*

But the cell that set my hand
To trembling while I wrote
Amen! lets go and dies.
I wait for the shadow
Below the cliff to bury
The choir of spilled rocks.

Then having, just for this scene,
Invented the sun's death,
I kneel in the wild grass
With nothing to deny.

VII   Labor and Tribulation

Flattening dough for pastry,
Thumping the high kitchen table,
My mother's forearms swelled
Like a bosun's. She hummed
Her girlhood tunes—"Love's Old Sweet Song,"
"The Long, Long Road A-Winding"—
Every surface, all odors charmed
To attend her rare good humor.

Her hair was white at thirty.
My aunt (her advisor, though younger,
And pretty, and always in trouble
Over men) would sit with her drinking
A bottle of Powers between them
On wet Sunday afternoons.
They worried about money, family.
Their voices would bring me from reading
To the room where they changed the subject.

Soon from her hospital bed
She was scolding me: *Mind yourself, now.*
In north-city slang, we joked
About half-forgotten troubles;

But she couldn't laugh as she used to,
Rocked by a giddy croaking—
One lung and most of the other
Gone: the family disease.

Not long after that we fought
Over money and didn't speak
For years; then I wrote from the States
And signed my childhood nickname. Soon
She was dead from too much whiskey
And pills and time to worry
About money, and illness, and about
Her thankless children, I suppose.

God of light and shadow,
Let her rest in my understanding.

VIII   Secret

What light painted
The ceiling with
Its map of cracks
And charted my path
Of sin and fear?
That must have been first light.

What age was I
When I could make out
The devil's wing
In the cracked plaster
Over my bed?
That was the age of unreason.

What sin occurred
While I was snug
In the warm bed
And my mother there

Warm in the dark?
No sin, no sin.

What fear tore
Through me when
I planted a row
Of green seedlings
In my father's garden
As he directed?
What fear when
They shrivelled, killed
By late frost? The fear
Of venture in a world of loss.

God of this new day
Set me free in your light
From this vain grief.

IX   Blessing

I will walk out today:
I will accept the shadow
Light casts for company.

I will walk out today,
Dry leaves, dry grass untroubled
By the shadow at my heel.

I will walk out today
With my children through the shadows
Of the wintry park.

They will play at hunting and hiding.
And when they grieve my going
This memory will bless them.

OWEN AT PLAY

Ex nihilo, Owen imagines, then contrives,
A world wherein he's sole Intelligence.
From Tinkertoy parts inert on the bedroom floor
He fuses wooden stars into galaxies.
In his own good time, these spiky suns
Will implode into characters—one-eyed, spiny, good
And bad—shoved about all their lives by huge
Incomprehensible grubby hands. They divine
Meaning in their lives only as seething breath,
Some celestial sheriff in his fury,
From whose own clumsiness both good and bad
May earn a beheading, or dismemberment;
Or, when he is merciful, oblivion.

That whisper's a portent: whom he would destroy
He renders helpless first with pricks and smarts.
Next, discord. Then anguish and terror spread
Indiscriminate through the frail universe.
Behold, not one bright block on another! Lo,
The *Realpolitik* of the Crackerjack animal circus!
Weep for the fingerpuppet, crammed before
Its time in a jigsaw box, whose pieces have long
Dispersed like holocaust atoms, God only knows where.

Wouldn't the Mother of God herself cry out
To him to cease and desist from this wrathful harvest?

Inscrutable lawgiver, turn from your terrible labor!
Put off the Apocalypse; bestow on this chaos
The order only you can perceive, and leave
The world to sleep in your sabbatical peace.

THE PICTURE OF LITTLE RORY
IN A MUNICIPAL PARK

Saxe Point, Victoria, B.C., January, 1975

Weary Rory dawdles on the path
Beneath the cedars where the light is dim,
As in ancestral caves. A bramble tugs
His sleeve, his face pale in the green shade,
Flanked by shards of fern, embraced by thorns—
Unlikely alabaster cherub in the wild
Greenery of a Douanier Rousseau—
He's no more my child than anyone's. Behind him,
A massive boulder looms, the tumbled head
Of a crude colossus, hewn by the torpid ice
A million years ago.
                I've turned, prepared
To call *Hurry up!*—but again I'm in the wrong
Place for fathers, under these boughs reduced
To a superfluous attendant. Now the light
Is fading quickly, threatening more snow;
And I've lost perspective. Rory, motionless
This moment in the whispering palace of cedars,
Is untimely pensive, as Velasquez made
His Infanta in the scene where dog and dwarf,
Maid of honor, the artist himself, are all
Stopped by a premonition, in a room
As dark as the grove we're halted in.
                       I'll call
Across this little distance, and he'll come,
Slow as ice, footprint in melting snow
Small as a bird's, and beg to be carried home.

THE AUTOBIOGRAPHY
OF THE IMPOTENT MAN

"Rise, take up thy bed, and walk."
—John 5:8

I

My earliest memory? why, the lassitude!
The servant's spoon at my mouth, the long
Staring at my feet, the crude charts they made
Of their coverings, their stains relating where
I went and could not go. . . . The cutting reek
Of old piss, the dung-reek of my own bed—
My thighs scratching together when they carried me
Through the city to take the waters I had no faith in.

My father in his prime died of the plague,
Howling his soul's curse at the marble walls.
They tell me his name is in the chronicles
For his reforms after the wars. At thirty-seven
I inherited the cursed villa, and the green balm
Of its gardens, and his salaaming servants. Found
No treasure, though everyone said we were rich.

The sickness had by then drawn yellow skin
Tight to the bones of my arms and legs. The stench
Of a cow's belly cut open, of spewed offal, rose
From me while I lolled on satin and dreamt
The indolent movement of others swaying around me.

My servants feared the spirit of my father:
For a year or so, until they began to forget
His power, they fetched me down to the pool. Useless!

What a figure I must have cut in my silk swaddlings,
My head full of ideas, impressions; the pillow
Wearing the hair from the nape; my features a child's
Leathern mask for the game of "Beggars"—what
A spectacle we made at the pool, my Egyptians
Lifting me naked into the bubbling mire!

Free for a while afterward from my own stench,
I could lie in the garden, steeped in a cloud of birdsong,
And burst a grape on my palate with my tongue,
Numbness on numbness; yet the sweet grape burst,
And its juice filled my throat while old Lares told
His tales of champions on horseback with spear and shield
Doing battle for the Pharoah and his Princess.
The clamor and flash of the events he told were as strong
For the brain as the grape as it burst on my tongue.

II

But old Lares with the rest forgot in time
My father's spirit pacing the echoing rooms.
I woke one morning, sunlight full on my bed,
So bright that the painted figures on the wall,
The plump daemonic dancers, seemed to cavort
Alive in the ritual grove. Silence. The air
Waited to tremble with pipes, with naked feet
Drumming on naked earth. My four senses
Tortured me with this silence. They had fled
At last, and stolen even the sacred lamps
From the altars. What fear must have gone with them!
Why had they waited so long? And yet, how timely!

Three silent days. Then a gang of slaves,
Freed by age or disease from their masters, crept
Through the villa like spiders. They found me swathed
In lambswool and satin, so thirsty I couldn't talk,
Except in a hoarse grunt. This way I pleaded all day;

And after dark, the two strongest carried me down
To the Street of the Angel's Pool, where I could beg
For scraps and live with the other stinking beggars.

III

A child of ten, no more,
Sores on arms and legs,
Stuffed hard crusts in my mouth.
She watched my tongue as an owl
Watches the young in her nest.
I choked down the rough crumbs.
Straw for a bed, like the beasts.
A long dying, before the miracle.

IV

To feel at my heels the smooth stones,
The slime on the walls, the oily waters
Breaking brown on my brown skin—how strange!
The coarse cloth between my fingers, the scabs
On old sores, the dizzy business of standing—
Strange! Pain clambers along this tree
Of nerves that grows from my heels into the old
Head that nods queerly at the body's news—

Tongue clatters its new consonants
As grapes would burst against my teeth. I hold
Another, limp, yellow, genderless, in my arms
As my slaves held me; and I lower him
Into the waters. He has hope. How soon
My whole being grows into its movements!

DEATH OF FATHERS

for Ken McCullough

His plane exploded
In oily black and red
On the Persian desert:
A dusty crescent of mountains
Wheeling in the periphery;
The tawny ground veering up.

This dream overtook any other;
I woke up sweating and shaking
To stare at myself while I shaved,
Slow to focus on my own face.

Every detail severely familiar:
The instruments warping and cracking,
The roar of flame in the cockpit;
His stern frown, one arm raised
To see better, unbelieving;
The ground reeling through the fuselage.

What reason have I to believe
He died as he wanted to?

My mother took to the madhouse;
His mistress knelt discreetly
At the back of the church for the service.
My uncles, my brother, and I
Brought the coffin with ashes
Gathered from the desert

To the family grave. It was all
Acted out with the proper restraint.

I'm cold enough now to let
This elegy rise between us.
All that time, every detail
Has remained as clear as a curlew's
Call in the night: he still
Grips the useless controls;
The unchanged ground spins up.

THE ARTIST, RECLINING

She leans forward; he is lying exhausted
After their making love. His head, at ease
In her lap, is careless and quiet for once,
The star fixed in a clear sky, waiting
        For its name.

When he turns his head to kiss her breast,
Her heartbeat rises to his lips, the language
For a whole history of art. Renoir,
Brush fastened to his wrist, would make
Her lean forward like this, and then describe
With easy, luminous strokes, his gratitude
        For the making.

HOUSE BURNING DOWN

What fire feeds on is mostly air, but I dwell
On what I own, how bitterly I'd start over.
Flame leafs through a shelf of books in minutes;
The pages swell into rippling levels of yellow.

Hoses curl from the engines to the men
Who lean back from the seething jets, the glare
On their faces like saints beholding a vision.

The busy lapping inside that unfixed roar
Holds to a staunch pattern. I draw closer
Through my fear. If only I could command
Fire, the oldest language, our mother tongue!

Now books and shelf are one. Flame sheathes
The roofbeam. To a great shout of timbers, the house
Leans inward. The doorway conjures a seamless
Red and orange curtain for the vanishing rooms.
Fire smiles in the teeth of a cellar window,
Then pours a firmament of sparks into the sky.

Flames chatter to each other, a fierce lingo.
I turn my back to recall the names of objects
Liquified by flame: *book, lamp, table, chair.*

And on my way home I call a blessing
On every sleeping house against the black
From which the yellow flame will soon depart.

THE EXILE, EN FAMILLE

Among my own, I'm a figure of fun,
A bare-fanged clown even in anger.
When I'm half-asleep over a new Theory,
Or consumed by fury at the day's ration
Of lies and theft in high places, they mock
Generously. I've learned to pay them
No mind. Without contempt, my children
Ignore my directions, my household rules,
Their nerves tuned to a frequency
That transmits but won't receive.
For their part, they burden me with such
Trivial tasks, oiling a hinge or putting up
Storm windows while my head is filled
With keeping a ketch's bow into the wind
Or listening to Brahms and Tolstoy talking
As they stroll a riverbank—I accomplish
Their love at small cost. As the trout
Leaping from the pool in the willow shade
Needs the deadly air to remind him
Of his element, and would not forego
The glistering arch he rises through,
I understand, while I fit the window
Into its frame, they give me
Their love at small cost.

AFTER YEATS, AFTER RONSARD, PACE *HOPKINS*

When we've been divorced for a while, and you get
Edvard Munch postcards from the Netherlands,
And late-night calls to check whether we're still friends
(Your eyes closed, your changed lips ruefully set

Against forgiveness; yet lending a canny ear),
You'll recall my forecast: how these walls
Will hiss their own surly silence, when what galls
Is neither my presence nor absence. Ah, my dear,

You'll finally come looking for me, checking the bars;
I'll be easy to find; you'll curse me, but I'll pay
No attention, thinking *She's old and grey.*
So, stay by this glowing fire, and thank your stars!

HABITATIONS

I

The fire's gone down: burnt pine
Leaves its pungent etching on the air.
With the house to myself like this,
And the room beginning to chill,
I can feel the plateau rise
Under great swatches of snow, and
Tilt up into the Cascades;
And beyond, the grey Pacific. . . .

The record is back in its sheath.
The melody from Brahms, the slow
Movement of the first concerto
For piano, lingers, hesitates.
If I exhale, it is gone,
Like a radio signal fading
Over great distance. Already,

Out over the drifted snow,
A long sound has filled
The expanse of moonlit air:
The coyote's sheer keening,
The high vowels of loss.

II

In this trance before sleep
I am nineteen again.

I have just switched off
The late-night jazz from Holland.
A lorry on the hill
Outside the Santry house
I'd never cared to live in
Grinds its gears, hauling
Hay to the city market.

On those nights, road sounds
And the blast of plane engines
Revving in maintenance hangars
At the airport would lend
That house its only substance.

III

Mother, sisters, brother,
Sleep tonight in the memory
Of those rooms, the frayed rugs,
The scarred mahogany furniture,
The hallstand mirror filling
With ghosts caught by the headlights
Of the traffic from Belfast.

One sister's hair spreads out
On the pillow like a mermaid's
In the tide; the other sighs
Like an opera heroine.
My brother, even in sleep,
Wears his anxious frown.

My mother is lying awake:
She rustles a page of her book.
My father is absent again:
His Grumman on the oily Orinoco

Roars out for take-off
And shudders into the air.

❖

The stairs creak with my weight.
Last to bed, I turn off lights.

ASTRONOMY

My head, this wrinkled planet,
Keeps emitting a garbled message.
Cells die and dissolve in the other
Galaxies—Abdomen, Wrist,
Larynx, Aorta, Eyelid,
And lonely remote little Penis.

God stretches, yawns, turns His back.
Black holes drink the stars where He was.

The
  Exile's Book of Hours
              1982

PRELUDE IN DARKNESS

Veni, Deus. Old ideas, like stairs,
Climb between me and a clear concept
Of the divine: I wait for a call
I fear won't come. Nothing personal,
Marcus Aurelius, but what's left
Is no more than the split hairs

Between the unknowable Absolute
And the mannish divinity
You Ancients lent to marble.
In our time, it is comparable
To a clear connection between, say,
Detroit and Dresden. You know the fruit

Of prayer is a mouthful of dry seeds.
Those moments devoted to saying over
Worn phrases, fingering smooth beads,
Dismal litanies of our daily needs,
Could be given to, say, praising a lover
While you helped her into her coat. Creeds

Are ramparts Reason's raised
Out of the slop and dross
Of unspoken feeling. *Can we get on,
Your Holiness?* Ego rasps: then
Strings and brass aspire; the chorus,
Uncertain, then sings praise.

SHORT JOURNEYS BEFORE DAYBREAK

I am the amber-eyed black
Cat who forsakes her species
To curl in the widow's lap.

I am jackal: can change places
With any beast of the griping
Night-chorus. I am colorless, faceless.

I am mollusc: without will, gaping,
I wait for the sea, my lover,
To change through me, a soft gasping.

I am hawk. A speckling moves. I hover,
Dive. A thin scream escapes.
I strike and strike. Will this end? Never.

I am bear, wrestling clumsily with my hopes.
Sleep is my oldest friend; I have one other.
When resentment straightens me into a corpse,
I lie with the Prince of Lies: man, stepbrother.

DAYBREAK

Newstime! Rise! Shine! Shake a leg!
Neuroses! Nemesis! Behold, I bring
TV tidings! What's a fad? What's a drag?
Outrage over coffee, of thee I sing—
Sex fiends, bigots, cartels, murderous falange—
My lungs boil, my guts fret for revenge.

Vanity, old deathshead friend, old bore,
Comes to chat while I shave and shiver.
A masque ensues, behind the fogged mirror.
I want, offstage voice announces. *Chancer,
Who d'you think y'are?* comes Ego's answer.
This can go on all day, hour after hour.

Contrast: black ellipses
Spread in soft new snow.
My children's path to school.
New light, a gold mist, blesses
Their going. Such moments, so few,
I take to heart, God's own fool.

EARLY MORNING WALK TO WORK

Turn off the boob-tube, take an ulcer pill.
Brouhaha! The sun is over the hill,
The cat is cleaning his fur on the warm sill.
Sing *Brouhaha!* Turbulent, damnable Will!

Go, my soul, patrol the patio
Between the theatre and the studio
Where speech and clay, player and potter prepare
To give the word its flesh, palpate mute air.
What news? What news? Tell me, Horatio.

LATE MORNING TALK
My Students Refuse The Craft

Away   away   this allure
    this yearning East   *appassionato*
inevitably takes you
    (our fond joke)   over

The unseen line   the *taboo*
    whatever way you turn   however
yearning   you feel the Self burn
        down to zero
desire   you cannot spurn
    gravity in one clap
rolling the flat map
    up   into a globe

Passing all   understanding   a lobe
    of sand   a tropic   latitude
surrendering   its name   Gratitude

Now   whatever course   is drawn
    west is true   already known
you are free   go   the same
    invisible way   every island   artless
        lying   prone
ocean steppingstones   on your charts
    all the blue   way home

NOON APOCRYPHA

In the Forenoon I rose up
                & went into hiding from my Life.
In the Midst of heavy Routine,
                whilst I partook of Coffee & a Smoke,
It was borne in upon me
                how vain & futile the whole Thing was.
My Guts they were aflame in their Acids
                & my Brows they burned with Insomnia.
For mine Enemies have encamped about my sore Brains.
Lo, my five Sons all in a bad Dream
                have been estranged of me,
Following hard on the Departures of their Mothers,
Who, in their several divorced Tongues
                have cursed me,
And lamented in a Chorus
                their Unhappiness with me,
Though I have betaken mySelf
                unto a Lifetime of Striving for their Sakes.

Yea, have I labored to placate these inconsolable Women,
In Tribulation & Turmoil,
                all for five Minutes' Affection:
The purblind hasty Rutting
                on the quaking Bed; the ammoniac Reek;
The oystery levelling Lovemuscle;
                the bleak Sheets
That after such Sessions of hard Bargaining
                bore my Signature.

For I am weary of my Life
                & would fain walk from it,
Or rise from this aching Dream,
                or sink into dreamless Sleep,
Yea, even at Day's noon Height.

MEDITATIONS OF AFTERNOON

I   De Mortuis . . .
    (Frank Stanford, John Berryman,
    Anne Sexton, Stanley Cooperman . . .)

Is it good in broad day to reflect on death?
The tricked brain's fused circuits, despair's stale breath—
Who can grasp the particulars? For example,
The young poet who sank from his gun, from a simple
Surfeit of powers—what generous, tender psalm
Evoked, but could not reveal, death's mysteries?
He wrote of his boyhood on the levee, becalmed
In sunlight. I recall a summer's ebbtide beach:
Shells gleam, strange tokens of a power beyond reach.
Neither his death, nor the slight catastrophes
Of my slow going, count for more on the globe
Than, for example, the gnat caught in the trembling web.

II   Interlude, with Alter Ego

Waxwings gather along thin phonewire:
Notes from an unfinished score.

Sing, ye choruses, sing out
Upon late sunlight's sloping glare.

Sing, soulmate soloist, silvervoice!
Had I your gift, your delicate air,

I'd raise the spirit from its mire of doubt,
Singing *Alleluia!* and *Rejoice!*

III Catnap, with Nightmare

What comes here? Splenetic,
Accursed old Ego, never
Satisfied, vaults and tumbles
From behind drawn stagecurtains
(Pink-and-gold brocade, embroidered
With masks and timbrels). Upright,
He grins and feints, urgent, tough
(Proscenium arch of plaster
With garlands and grinning sylphs),
Gestures, exhorts, then insults
In Russian or Kurdish. I lean
Forward to catch the meaning.
But the conductor has raised
Big stubby hands
Over the hidden orchestra
(Trumpets, cymbals, a fierce drumming)
And Ego, bent at the waist,
Mutters ingratiatingly.
Agued and stern, he holds
His cropped head (clap hand,
Clap hand, till silence comes home).

LATE AFTERNOON, RUNNING:
CLOSE REASONING, LISTENING CLOSELY

Lift me, God, from the Self's diurnal fussing,
That I may see the futility of paper,
The nagging transience of plan and project,

The insensate beggary of every object
I cling to: show me each in true and proper
Relation—though I feel I may be addressing

You, God of this blank white world, as an abstraction.
Some say you are Nature, and Law is your reflection;
Others disparage, murmuring you are Absolute
Zero, cosmic comedian; other beliefs too rash,
Even for me—too finite—though, irresolute,
I long for One who gives clay life, words flesh.

Infinite God, I pray in the terrible glimmer
Of your perfection, what is your secret will?
Like King Claudius, I feel faith grow dimmer,
Heavier with the world's weight: I could fulfill
Yet a strategem, claim a small victory. . . .
Lift me up, God, into your mystery!

SUNSET

My children make their way home,
Dragging their feet through the snow.
A robin lets one note fall
Through muted air. God, how can I know
You? Light retreats. The cold hour has come
For surrender. Why should it ravel

My every sense to mouth this word? To call
Above the clamor of the will to some
Mighty impression of you, sacred foe
Whose image we design and limn and frame
After our own—and with such brazen skill
We claim an intimacy, bathe in the afterglow

Of your immense absence! God, I grow
Weary of guess, and would yield all
The ground I hold against the mortal claim
You make on me, if you would once reveal
Yourself with a clear sign. Then I would go
On my knees repeating your right name

In prayer; and you would be as a footfall
Leaving its dark impression on the snow,
Leading me at last the true way home.

New
  Poems
  1982–88

for Deirdre,
love

A GESTURE

Your fingers can dart
Out like scared snipe
From their nest in your lap,

And your hair, a furled wing
At your temple, can wait
For light itself, as air
Stays for bird, cloud, seed.

When you are this near,
A startled bird in my throat
Flourishes—the fear
Attendant on miracles.

Flight's little secrets curve
Into these fingers: I swoop
Home to the nest, a smart hawk.

TEN-MILE RUN

FIRST MILE

A red-tailed hawk
Lifts from a pole
Into hard blue air;
Scouts the stubble,
Then swoops up quickly,
Stops those big wings
And alights, brown
On a brown pole, further
Down the blue air.

Three times he loops
Forward, pole to pole,
Slurring his consonants
Over the stubblefield.
Then he wheels back
To where he began. The field
Is all his: I keep
To the road, the highpitched
Conversation between
Distance and time.

UPHILL

Two murderous thugs
Sledge at each other
In the alley between lungs.

There are quicker ways,
But murder keeps its pace.

Sisyphus on hell's hill, death-
Cheater, teach me hills.

DOWNHILL

Feet clap roadmetal: lakes
Of stubble float away
Entirely on their own power.
Parts of the body
Which haven't spoken for years
Greet each other amiably:
Hello, Instep! Good day, kind Knee!
Finch and thistle converse.
Acacias on a far ridge
Trace a Gothic parliament
For coyotes, whose business
Is loping—who am I to go
Stealing along their side
Of the road? They'll swear out a writ
And the road will turn for the worse.

THIRD MILE

Off left in a hollow
Three farmhands round
A tractor slide from view.

A stiff little tableau,
As Breughel would have it.
Three magpies plot

Against the men, restless
In black and white, ready
To rob them of noon repose.

Cloudless blue air and plowed
Brown earth. You and I, friends,
Have common ground, but our ends

And means differ. . . . No need to debate.
Here unplowed stubble climbs
Right to the road's edge. I turn

Uphill again, grateful to leave you
Itching at the corner of vision.

FIFTH MILE

The air I breathe in
Is kissing-cousin to the air I let go.
The air I let go takes shelter
In the shade with the deer and hare.

Finches in thistles are flirting
With the air I breathe in and away.

The breath I let go just now
Goes to flirt with thistledown, birdwing.

The air I breathe now
Makes it worth letting that breath go.

SIREN

Blonde hair flows over her shoulders;
She raises a hand in greeting
From the door of her mobile home.
She wears only a flimsy kimono,
Her bosom seismic with perfume.

"Rest here," and her hip leans,
Her mouth poses a moist kiss,
Her eyes signal, "Rest here,
Rest here," she sings, the wind sings,
Passing the shadowy door.

But the heels of the wily runner
Play a different tune on the road.
Here at the base of the hill,
He can see the right way home.

NINTH MILE

The right foot lets
The left know
Too much. Every rib
Asks its separate
Question:
 What leads?
What follows?
 What is?
That wasn't.
 It is.
It can't be.
 It can.
It can't.
 It's gone.
It can't.
 Gone now.
It's gone.

NEAR THE FINISH

Numb. The limit of sin
Meets the grin of good.
All matter's forward motion.

Sin's limit is knowledge.
The limbs have learned
That what resists

Persists by yielding.
Extremities no longer
Report their positions:

So much for knowing
How far you can go.
Mind floats in a selfless daze,

Admiring its mirror image:
Breath, afloat in veiled
Silence. Senses suspended,
A dry joy perpetuates.

AOR* AGAINST THE INGRATE
WHO ABUSED OUR HOSPITALITY

"Nor certitude, nor peace, nor help for pain. . . ."
—Matthew Arnold

I

Here on the vast edges drear
Of the continent where you've flown
From our poor isle's naked shingles
To gain time and peace for the work,
We give you welcome and shelter,
Though you knew before you accepted
And you know as you arrive—
Olympian, jovial, brave
As you take up your position—
We can't help you, brother.

II

You've mastered the bleak art of Changes:
Now you leave aside our agreement
To masquerade as Lost Soul.
In the stories you've culled from your life,
You've insisted the world must suffer
With you its night of pain:
Godforsaken rooms
And blighted streets more strangely
Cursed than even this town, a scab
On the dry side of Purgatory,

*An old Gaelic form, meaning "lampoon, satire, or personal attack" (Dinneen's *Irish-English Dictionary*)

Agreed—but it offers shelter.
As for this *malaise:*
We can't help you, poor soul.

III

From the burly give-and-take
Below decks, or on shoreleave, you learned
More than to sing, didn't you,
For your supper and a few hours
Of solitude? The impromptu parts
For clown, talebearer, victim,
Came to you easily, didn't they?
We can't help you, sailor.

You've learned other parts off by heart:
Cheap labor without a work-permit,
Your ship disabled in Galveston;
Starvation and prison in Asia;
Cheap talk in a Spanish *taverna.* . . .
Dirt and cheap clothes and heroin
In a Hamburg slum. Inasmuch as the least
Of these people did it to you,
Whole nations became your enemies.
At your worst, you're the blear-eyed trickster,
The cocky prophet sent among us
To provoke us into mean gossip.
We're *sorry* for you. Are you deaf?

IV

Now you lean over suicide's precipice
Till a few murmurs reach you: *Ah, don't.*
This you take for applause.

Now the Wronged Artist—what an act!
What a go-boy you are—what a chancer!
Every favor you accept as your due;
You judge us all in the fixed
Lens of your own condition,
Immured in trickery, neck-deep
In bad luck and cosmic sorrow.

We murmur, *Ah, don't*. We can see
You shivering in fear behind
That bloodless mask, liar.
We can't help you, liar.

V

Go on, stir up your tiresome wavelets
Of slander, and believe you arouse
A storm of consequence. Play Victim,
Nine-Days'-Wonder, Hop-O'-Me-Thumb,
Every smart act you've a mind to.

Now, climb back aboard the big jet,
Home to cloudy misery, to the one pal
Who'll share his bed, your end
Compassed round by the humorless tattle
You chatter like a tame marmoset,
Your chain stretched full.

May you drown in the blood-rose pool
Of your tireless self-pity! We can forgive
Your lies, your tricks, your capers,
But not your unflagging contempt.
We too have work on hand, and you
Wasted our time. Get going,
You bastard. We can't help you.

N.Q.

IN THE RED CORNER

for Jim

In a storm of voices, a voice
Is calling, *Don't think—move!*
Disappointment is at your ribs
Too early. Hands hardly your own
Grow heavy, impatient. Too slow,
You watch him from heavy eyelids.
Breath gears down. A wheel slips
And grinds under your heart. You block
Hard blows with a forearm, and shift
Your feet—left; back. This is art.

A rose springs in your head.
Stay, you hear. *Keep him close.*
Salt stings your underlip.
Huge globes weave, gleaming red.
You punch blunt air. Pain sears
One eye. You catch his dancing shadow
In a corner, and go to work. Sweat
Splays from your glove like fireworks.
His blurred mask ducks under a red
Fist. Pains carve out a space
Under the shoulders. Down here, I feel
Those aches gouge too. This is love.

Heat roars down this well
Of rope and canvas. Quicklime
Burns high in the craw. But these
Wise pains advise you: *Keep*
On him. He dances in circles. Watch

Him slow and blink. The weight
Your hands must lift can be no more
Than his. When he dances, keep steady,
And when he's steady, dance. Win or lose,
Raise those arms at the end,
And be dancing. This is praise.

THE NUN OF ST. MICHAN'S

Among the bodies preserved in the crypt under
St. Michan's, a tenth-century Dublin church,
is that of a thirteenth-century nun,
aged about twenty-four at her death.

for Joanne and Ruben Trejo

This, this is God's will.
I repose in my narrow box
Of cracked deal; my head turned
Aside this way, not from shame,
Though my poor brown shroud
Long ago shredded to dust, and you,
Pilgrim, who climb down
Where the dry air keeps our bodies
Without corruption, can see
My sex, this portal of bone
And coppery skin, which caused
Me great shame while I strove
To keep my vows and live
According to God's will.

On the morning I was made
A chaste Savior's Bride,
They cut away the child's
Few fair locks from my head
And dressed me so no mortal man
Would tempt me, or be tempted.
Prostrate on the flagstones
At the altar in my white surplice,
I surrendered all my worldly
Powers, and vowed to obey
The Abbess's rule; to keep my body
A pure gem for Mary's Crown,

Intacta; to own nothing, but to give
My labor in penance for the world's sins.

Then I put on the coarse brown
Garment that would be my shroud,
And joined our little company.
We chanted God's praise at all hours,
In the glow of many candles, willing
Captives of the Holy Spirit.

But soon my own body betrayed me.
The Devil of Night tore through me,
A black spasm of torture and release—and sleep,
O sleep brushed my face with his wing,
My hands fluttered like wings,
I wept that Christ my bridegroom
Would not forgive my weakness
And drive him away from me, this demon
Who chuckled and snored in the throats
Of my sisters as they lay in their cots!

Between labor and prayer
In our little chapel, silence.
I tried, as my confessor
Bid me, to look on the Cross,
To contemplate His wounds,
His Blood our healing wine,
His Body our bread of grace.
But often half swooning I dreamt
Of Him borne down to me
As any bride would have it.
How was this God's will?
Prayer perished on my lips.
Then the day's round, an expiation
For past sin; for sin
I knew I would yield to.

On my knees where I scrubbed the kitchen hearth,
In the field where I tended the meagre wheat,
On the bog where I lifted the basket of turf
For the fires, I begged to be rid of this flesh
That would corrupt all my thought. But God
Answered no prayer of mine. Christ died
For my sins, but would not redeem me from them.
So, as His widow in my coarse smock and hood
I knelt in the mud by the Liffey and thumbed out
The few roots that would flavor our meal. It seemed

Scarcely a moment after my eyes closed
On the dizzy water, the clouds in an uproar,
That I heard my sisters chirping like mice
And I so cold, and the bog's fragrance
And strange grunted prayer as they carried me
Back to my cell. Was it all
A dream, those years, psalms,
Beeswax, rosaries, the sins of my flesh,
Stroke upon stroke of the switchbroom over
The convent floors, until that sinking down
To lie stretched full by the river in surrender?

Because the power of flesh
Could waken me into wedlock
With Christ's bodily form
As I contemplated His Cross,
And God answered no prayer of mine,
I turned my head aside
With my last strength when the Abbess
And her priest urged me to kiss
His crucified flesh; and breath
Left me at last to this quiet,
This brown unaging stillness,
Intacta. This is God's will.

AOR AGAINST THE TERMAGANT
FROM CALIFORNIA WHO
CONFUSED INSTRUCTION
WITH INDIGNATION

The cats. One ashen, head and neck of a mantis,
The other stubtailed, sooty, distraught haunches.
They looped round the apartment, ugly as sin,
Sniffing the awkward furniture, the monastic bed.
"Just like your cell in San Francisco, Mother,"
Spoke out the son, couragemonger, rooting through
His brains for the *mot juste*. Mother had done time
For riot in '68—a seventy-year-old handful then,
"Free Speech! No More War!"—such glorious battling
When, as incongruous as Catherine the Great,
She took on the cops in the fervent street.

She lost one cat the coldest night of winter.
It turned up a few days later, lisping malice,
Not stiff in a snowdrift as she'd envisioned it,
But rescued and pampered by steamplant boilermen.
She wailed her Maenad grief into her vermouth;
Her vicious pet might just as well have croaked.
Already she was plotting the fiction of her ordeal
Among us—that celebrated knack of twisting truth
Into little devotional beads of hate.

Two women, one leadpipe larynx, one kohlrabi hair,
Signed up for her seminar and occupied
The front seats, popping stupid questions.
This deadpan Queen of Hearts in Academe
Matched their gall: spat back
A humorless polemic, the soul dressed up
In one seamless, ageless tantrum, a two-tone

Falsetto that curled even fighting words
Into complaining whines—"Speak Out! It's Wrong!"
She kept her grip on outrage, the constant fuss
She brought from Ohio when she ran off as a lass.

At dinner, no quarter. She'd argue the hind legs
Off the chair you sat in, her comfort a case against you.
She'd badger you to be active, to join campaigns;
Or her cheerless eyes would fix on the evening news,
Glaring at jowly foes in Washington.
Absurd Medusa, earrings of dead-white bone,
If only she could, she'd turn us all to stone.

Queen Mother of Dismay, she'd try the patience of Job.
She clutched her outrage and pain as a bad-mannered child
Grips her bag of sweets and whines for more.
Her dearest friends have learned to smile, hug, kiss,
And doubt her every word. So hard! So stoic! So wronged!
Ungrateful mewling dowager, you kissed us goodbye
When your baffled son packed you in the car for home;
Yet, with that feline sneer you're noted for,
You dismiss as a weakness all affection and care.

The fame you craved from childhood is a garland
Withered to dust. Remembered arms of lovers
Sear you like chains. You were Circe, never Penelope,
Never lovely, never free, a sinewy libertine
Who suffers now the hell of your own regret.
Satisfied or not, the revenge you sought
Has blighted your soul and dulled your sunniest hour.
Here's our parting gift, whether you want it or not:
Our pity goes with you, wherever the hell you are.

                                    K.B.

WHAT THE RECENT SURVEY HAS REVEALED

Gathered at random, like extras, the figures effect
A curious passive murmuring, to project
The multitude's doubts and fears. No one seems to direct

The production, but there's a plot: servants bend
Over guests at a great banquet, a lovely blonde
Approaches through marble columns, blood from a wound

Spreads on a silk shirt. . . . But then, one nagging flaw—
A courtier's New World slang, say—and we withdraw
Credence from the "authentic," so expertly conveyed,

So carefully scripted; and the whole show—
The speeding carriage, the plaster colonnade,
The whole cast of thousands—could, for all we care,
Go up with the plywood palace in the final fire.

RUNNING IN SNOW

From the roadside the undersides
Of boughs and cornices blacken
To my liking. The sky drifts
My way, and melts on my lip.

Ache, ache, little bird
Hiding under my shoulder.

Where have my footsteps gone?
A mile or more slipped away
Since I heard their steady tapping
Lead me through the hush.

Snow has filled each step.
Yet a dark track pulses
Just out of sight. A pheasant
Mocks from a whitening field.

Steady, steady, bird
Twittering in my throat.

The void spins round behind,
Above; draws me upwind of silence.
Particle by particle, the world
Blindly remakes itself.

Quiet, quiet, bird
Hopping on the ridge of my spine.

High Drive whirls into a silvery nothing.
Hangman Valley's a muffled rumor.
A car passes, quiet as cancer;
One headlight eats into the sky.

Houses gather in their streets
Like museum displays. Traffic
Thickens, murmuring through
Swirling veils, dead slow.

Sing, sing, little bird
In your cage under my shoulder.

Mansions, domes, cathedrals
Appear and dissolve. I have come
Through our galaxy, atom by atom:
My home could be anywhere.

Sing, sing, little bird.

SPOKANE PERSPECTIVE

for Carolyn Kizer

For blocks the derelicts
Drop back behind one another,
Glass gone from the windows,
To a billboard by the freeway.
Beyond that, the pines rise,
A poised green *tsunami*.

The scene requires no motion
But the pigeons fidget anyway
On the parapet of a warehouse
Dolled up as a Renaissance villa
Powdered by wheatfield dust.

Developers ransacked history
For that *décor*—Gothic France,
The Moors, Tudor England—to furnish
Their Inland Empire with an aspect
That would outlast the sceptics.

The lights change one after the other
The length of the half-empty street:
Red to green, red to green, red to green
Retreats like a disappointed
Prospector from Saturn.

Not a building in view where anyone
Takes calls in a cluttered office
Or scolds a subordinate, or pauses

At a window, to regard the restive
Pigeons. Look out past the freeway:

Don't you want those pines
To sweep in over the whole damned city?

AOR AGAINST THE BAD REVIEWER

Rigid and bald as a dead rat's tail,
For you all meat must taste and smell dogshit.
You dribble opinion like slop from a pail:
Mean spirit, weak prose, weaker wit.

When you're in your narrow grave and stinking,
These lines are all you'll be remembered for.
Better to rot forgotten, you'll be thinking,
Than this memorial to the snivelling cur you are.

D.S.

COMING & GOING

Look, how we curl into sleep after love:
Our bodies are so content, they convey
No more sense than a pair of gourds
In a Cézanne *Nature mort*, or a tableau
Of Beckett—when a brushstroke or a sigh
Allows for shapes that may not have been there.

In this way, our spirits have climbed out
To stroll the Cerulean, where
Time and space are one. While form
Is a mere memory, our souls

Dance, those sleeping husks so far
Removed that being without matter makes
Clear sense.
           Now light attends
The window, to give flesh its due.
Thigh at hip and head on breast, we wake.
And when that dance plays out, we'll take
Our ease in heaven, just like this.

THE EXILE'S FIFTH SYMPHONY

ALLEGRO VIVACE

Out of the zero under sound, the pure
Dark spinning through unseen galaxies,
The stuttering instruments chart
These four notes: can you hear them?

Note answers note—can you hear how the planets
Spin round with our spinning globe?
Can any human spirit answer? What would we hear?
Would we learn of a beginning or an end?
These are the chords: can you hear them?

Can you with these voices, these four notes,
Call up in joy or pain a memory
To make our music worth its pain, its joy?
Play these four notes: who will hear them?

SCHERZO

These rising chords
Will dance in time
To flute and oboe
Twining through
The *continuo*
Of viols as doves
Weave through shadows
When clocktower bells
Clang out at noon
In the sunny piazza
Where lovers have danced

To blithe tunes
And woven a silvery
Column of pure light
Out of shadows. Memory
Glitters, spins; the tempo
Quickens, four notes
Repeated. Listen. Look.

ANDANTE CANTABILE

The sweaty redfaced laughter of drunken friends!
They bawled and sang and called farewells; the street
Filled with their cries and snatches of song, and the stars
Climbed above the old bitch-city I loved and left.

The long train hauled its burden of lights
West across the shady lowlands, and unravelled
One wavering note over the villages. Meadows
Grew purple at dusk; but a pale ribbon stayed
All along the horizon, where the black bones
Of withered trees saluted our chain of lights
As we rolled and rattled to the western sea.

ALLEGRO MODERATO

And although that music curved
To weave those scenes into the cloth
It made of night, let it change
To a swift barrage, a climb and dive,
And memory is blessed or mocked
According to the way you hear those notes.

Of these four images, harmony is made,
Even as they fade against the light:
A bowl of chrysanthemums, each bloom
A bronze fist raised at mortality;
A blade of grass, black in the amber gem;

Stars of frost that melt on a winter window;
And you, with your head tilted to listen
For these four notes repeated, keeping their promise:

> Store this chain of notes,
> These woven images, until
> You learn what tapestry
> Death will unfurl in time.

PRESS CONFERENCE:
KING JAMES VERSION

from the Gospel According to St. Thomas

"Keep faith: you know he is with you."
                    We have questions to ask.
"He is here. He will speak with you."
                    He will give us only denials.
Aides and guards surround him. His hand shakes. He smiles
For the lights, brighter than sun, in which they bask.
Help our unbelief.
        "We have made it our task—"
The great room fills with meaningless cries.
"All stand please."
        What changes? Will he raise
Great armies, smite our foes?
                    His smile is a brazen mask.

They gather in the aging leader's views,
Which they will sift and weigh and set in store
By morning. He smiles. His head shakes. He brings good news.
His hands lift from the podium: The poor,
The army's power, the future, his wife's good cause.
He shrugs, he waves, he grins.
                    All are in his care.

AOR AGAINST THE PHILISTINE
WHO DESTROYED LOVELY DUBLIN VISTAS
WITH HIS UGLY ERECTIONS,
THEN ABSCONDED TO LONDON

Hello, little bearded squirrel-eyed fellow,
Wreckerball head in the fur and leather
And limpwristed how-d'you-do's
Of fashion's perfumed reception rooms—
This is your wake-up call from Dublin,
A call with a curse, you little hobgoblin.
You'd sink a shaft in the Florentine Baptistry
If they'd let you near it, you hapless catastrophe.

While your Christian Brothers imagination
Whirs and clicks out its imitations
Of Gropius and Frank Lloyd Wright,
We creep up on you to give you a fright,
Rising up from that bulldozed patch
Where the old city wall collapsed
On Wood Quay, thanks to your mean designs,
The blistered plans of your maggoty brains;
And we put bad cess on those monolithic
Lumps you stuck up on the banks of the Liffey.

Before your eyes while you are sleeping,
An ulcerous nightmare will keep you
Popping purple tranquillizers
That match the color of your eyeballs.
All that ferro-concrete mass,
That bilious carbuncle of glistening glass,
Will fester and crack and quickly become
A tatty bureaucratic slum.

While high and low officials labor
To bring forth records and working papers
Seeking approval for this and that
And the office machines go rat-a-tat-tat,
From deep underneath your skimpy foundations
We will all rise up—ten generations
Of cornerboys touts and gurriers
Barrowmen barristers pimps and criers
Tycoons turnkeys bailiffs—all
Scoundrels like you, Crown Prince of Gall.
Our chatter will travel from level to level
To rattle your twin towers of New Babel.

Fine dust will filter through a wide crack. . . .
Silt will sift and sigh and suck
At weakening pilings . . . floors will quake. . . .
Then down with the whole works, thunder and rumble—
Hundreds of minions will scramble in rubble
Like shrimp in a net—you will spasm, jerk, wake. . . .

We leave you to ponder with anguished deflation
The plans on your drawing board, and despair.
Though they've made you a fortune, those cheapjack creations,
You're still a plump nobody; and your greatest fear
Is our news-flash this morning: as sure as you're living in
Hopes of preeminence, you will die in oblivion.

S.S.

TENOR SOLO ON ST. CECILIA'S DAY

"The diapason closing full in Man."
　　　　　　　　　　　　—Dryden

Facing the humping flatfaced banks
Raised like cromlechs over their hoards,
We watch, from our innocent vantage over
Coffee, these two blue uniforms
Unloading bags of cash and boxes of bills
From a Brinks truck. They pile it all up
On a dolly, and haul. The bags tilt.
Two—three—tumble onto the sidewalk.
"Okay guys, don't shoot, we're just
Helping to keep the streets free of litter—"
We sing out our pious little joke
For the lawyers and brokers around us.
"Come on, do we look likely to do street crimes?"
They keep their noses in their coffee. No one smiles.

Next, my barber friend, the only one
I've ever known to play Rossini and Handel
In his shop, is passing the time of day
With me on the corner of First and Wall
When a fat citizen, new-moon smile
Over his paunch, announces, sure of his facts,
The phones are tapped, and They have us on Their computers,
Every dime and vice, and satellites
Beam on us always—then he crosses the street,
Roly-poly, careful to obey the WALK sign.
I'm putting Haydn's "Creation" on tape
From borrowed records when the Stormy One
Arrives from work, mad as the ghost
Of the great ancestor who scolds me

Constantly for chronic laziness.
A tiff ensues, a cloud no bigger
Than your thumb, that puts out the sun.
Weary talk about money, which, with sex,
The experts tell us, causes most
Disharmony in the home. As we fall
Asleep on our anger, which the experts tell us
Not to do, the good ship *Truth* clears port
With her cargo of accord. (How often
We see those riding-lights flicker and slip
Over the ambiguous horizon, without
Gaining the slightest idea what ship it was.)

Neither money nor sex the cause
Of the hard word and the silent frown,
But what we heard in the town,
Separately, in our different ways,
Through the static we'll never get used to:
A faint song over a great distance.

> The tide whispers in the ear
> Of the gleaming moon.
> Shorebirds in a line
> Riffle in light wind,
> Heads tucked in their wings,
> Along the ruined seawall.
> *Wunderbar,* Eve spoke,
> When she first beheld the world
> And our long exile began.

THE DYING SWAN

The piano ripples a delicate
Evocation of water; then the hands
Of the cellist, in the light
From the music-stand, form at the wrists
Into opposed heads, a kind of puppetry
Required to derive a *frisson* of mourning
From the instrument's long throat—and that figure,
Slight as mercury in its glass vein,
The weather's wisdom—a girl, a being in white,
Confined between the planes of floor,
Blue backdrop, and wings—conveys
Death's flight by winnowing her wrists. . . .
And we reflect on swans, on waters where they die
Into eternal blue. The girl lowers
Her feathered head to her white breast,
Opens a lifeless hand, and the light leaves her.
Afterward for hours the breath of meaning
Stirs the painted veils that memory
Has made of the dance and the cello's lament.
The movement of these figures throws a shadow
We take for truth, though it be no more than the swan-
Shadow anyone can make
By pursing the fingers and bending the wrist as you would
To draw the bow across the strings—if you can find
A white backdrop, and put yourself between it
And the light, and feel the swan's weather in the carotid.

AOR AGAINST THE WARMONGER

Look at the hands, kept out
From the sides, to draw his guns
On cue, as for thousands of takes
In those cowboy stand-offs.
He could still play bit parts
In those black-and-white campaigns
Where his side won every time.

He should groan without cease
From the small ancient pains that live
In his bowels; but he'd shrivel
Into a leathery foetus before he'd admit
To fear. He finds this code of use also
When marines die in their barracks,
One of the many fatal mistakes he lived through.

Look at him, hair a black cowl, as odd
As a bishop's mitre or a dowager's
Tiara, his tireless tongue
Chewing on those hoary lines:
This creature, this incomplete
Reptile awaiting fulfillment
In the wreckage of Eden. He'll keep
Coming back to life until he finds
A world befitting him. Picture

A sandy islet, the cobalt tropics.
The salty reek of shellfish. Wrinkled neck
Thrust out, head sideways, the aged iguana

Manoeuvres stiffly, blunt horny toes
Pushing through his own dung.
He lurches heavily forward, the forked
Tongue darting. Shrill seabirds
Dive on him. Maggots and lice
Rummage in the cracked rubbery skin.
This is the world war has given him.
This is the role we assign him,
To play this scene over and over
Until he understands and gets it right.

                              R.R.

POOL AT THE Y

Lawyers and salesmen muscled around,
Clanked locker doors, restive as sharks.

They rubbed and shrugged under the showers.
Pink or tanned, paunched or lean, they stood

As one kind with him, lashing themselves
With water, or drooping under the jets,
Steaming like beasts of burden.
  ❖
Light from high overhead swayed
On empty green water. After a boy

Jack-knifed from the low board, he eased
Into the flashy rippling, and was changed.

A girl with nothing to hide in her Lycra skin-suit
Sprawled in her chair and vaguely smiled.

In such a vaulted space, Virgins and Martyrs
Found a fortitude to live and die by,
Back in the Age of Sin.
  ❖
But here was the Age of Vigor. He pushed off
And thrashed out a length. Then back.

Chlorine scoured his eyes. He slowed and rolled
Down a green cheering universe, and back,

Stroke by stroke, shouldering the invisible
Rope of water, until he tired and climbed out.

The lovely lifeguard smiled upon water and light
Admiringly, and on him. But she stayed to keep watch

Over the other swimmers when the sauna's heat
Took him by the scalp and led him down
A single step, into the Age of Age.

THE PHOTOGRAPHER'S MODEL

He blurred the famous face in the first take.
They tried again: every time, something was wrong.
He gathered himself into his alpaca coat; turned
Her head this way and that with a fingertip;
Squinted; adjusted the focus; adjusted the light;
Bent to peep through the lens; bent frowning back.

And she, a pillar of impatience, shoulder and back
To him and his camera, proclaimed her mistake
In letting him have his way. She primped her hair. The light
Was his true mistress, who could always do her wrong
Simply by being. Now again the hard tip
Of a forefinger commanded her to turn

Into the overheated creamy glare, and return
To the camera's adoring stupor. At the back
Of the studio, a mirror aged her vaguely. On tip-
Toe, holding his coat to one side, he tried to take
Another reading. A truce held. Then, feeling wronged
By his absorption, she determined to find the light

Unbearable. "Please"—her hand a visor—"the light!"
Hands rammed in the pockets of his yellow coat, he turned
To the camera and called, "No, your soul is wrong."
What was the meaning of this? Shocked, she fell back
On the couch, betrayed beyond anger—and he took
Her photograph with an accidental tip.

The pose is too strong—she'd misunderstood him—and one tip,
After all the coaxing, the arranging of hair, the gauging of light,
Had set the dark eye to wink, the cloudy film to take
Her image: the creamy skin, one hand poised to turn
Away pain, one open on her lap to lure back
A certain lover, as if nothing whatever was wrong.

But irony, bridegroom of justice, can right no wrong.
He, whose betrayal made him unworthy to tip
The heel of her hand, is powerless to call back
The passing of her beauty into light,
Now featured in texts on portraiture, a turn
Of events for better or worse like a kiss. She takes

Her form from what he takes to be the wrong
Impression. Turn the page now; and take a tip
From fame: that light, once cast, cannot be taken back.

THE EXILE ON HIS FAILING VISION

Sandymount Strand, June 1982.
I.M.J.J.

I

Hup! I come to a halt, facing the sea. Count
Blessings. I can wait. In the holy hour I spent
Walking these tide-ribbed sands, my sight gave way
To something of the dazzling play between air
And matter, near and far, Howth and the bay,
Cloud and horizon, and the fugitive sun.

Light slanted down that wet sand, a benediction.
But the focussing muscles refused their function.
Sight had nowhere to go—could only skitter along
The sea's rim, jigging with sandpipers
And the little dancing waves of Sandymount.

Back the short stretch to our flat, I'm compelled
To go slow. Is this heart trouble? Wait.

II

Returned to desk and book, pad and pen, the eyes
Have their work cut out for them: clouds gallop
Over the print with a meaningless verve, like pups
Chasing their yapping shadows on the strand.

I concentrate, and try another page
Or two. I can wait. Words, words. What troops
Parade here, under what colors, pray?
Now comes a double image of a double image,

A shimmering misgiving, the print reduced
And edged by light. Sequence, consequence
Blink like stars; words glisten like cockleshells.
Sentences go past, waving, to the front;
Another paragraph pulls alongside, docks.

Consonants march out, two abreast. Hail, vowels!
A new page surrenders its odors of damp
Pulpwood and machine oil. The other senses,
They say, learn to serve better. I can wait.
Stars break under the eyelids. *His milde Yoak.*

III

The overgrown roses have speckled the granite sill
With crimson petals. Evening has taken all
But the topmost branches of the great sycamore.
Small clouds drift out to sea—a handful of petals
Thrown on a purple cloth. All heaven's treasure.

A pool on the strand this moment is as deep
As the advancing tide will let it be. Light waits
In its retina. Curlews call.
A dog splashes through, and the pool breaks
Into countless crystalline stars. The eye rescues
This image, remembering in its darkness

Youth could neither escape nor understand
Such play between impossible and possible.

THREE ACTS FROM A PLAY

I

For one season, much laughter: we learned to take
In our stride the age's age-old joke,
What we most desire, we must let go.
On the crucial evening, I sat through a show
While she sailed off, resolved, it seemed, to mend
What matters needed mending with her friend.
She trimmed her jib, though: leaving the theatre,
I found her, radiant as a changed character
Who remembers with delight the earlier scene
Which made change possible, with all its pain.

II

She opened the lower button of her blouse,
Pausing at a mirror as we left the house.
"Temptress," I called to her, as though in prayer.
"Not so," she said. "What, then?" "A woman's power."
Then, to divert me from that truth, she laughed.
But her perfume, at its body-temperature, left
No doubt she could rouse the four winds from their rest,
Or start the hero on his journey west.
"You explain all history," I replied.
Ever since, she's contentedly denied
She meant more by it than her smile. She must know,
By leaving that lower button open, how
She could command, from lover or passerby,
After surrender, lifelong loyalty.

III

Her womanhood collected into a pale
Version of herself waking up, a smile
Half-composed on her lips, as though to right
A wrong or heal the sick. "More light," I thought,
And flooded the room with it, to photograph
"The Lady Waking"—but she disturbed with a laugh
That paleness, that balanced moment, desire
Ready to be fulfilled. And now, the hair
Fashionably combed, she may go serene
Among strangers and friends, none of whom have seen
Child, girl, woman, all at once—
The spirit waking to our world of sense.

James J. McAuley was born in Dublin, Ireland, in 1936. Now a naturalized United States citizen, McAuley is a professor of English at Eastern Washington University in Cheney, Washington. The author of eight previous collections of poetry, a verse play, and a libretto, he lives in Spokane, Washington.